the Man for all time

for
Mark Sherritt Wilkins
with whom I share an anniversary

C. S. Mann

the Man
for all time

morehouse-barlow
new york

the Man for all time

contents

introduction

This book is an attempt to provide something which is not easily to be found at this time—a life of Jesus. It is difficult for us to understand the life of Jesus for two reasons. First, the kind of material which biblical scholars write as a result of their investigations tends to be confined to a number of periodicals not easily available to the average person, and it takes a very considerable time for the kind of things which scholars write to find their way to the general level of church people. Second, as church people we have become accustomed, through some illustrated lesson books and Bibles and some hymns, to material that is most unsatisfactory. Thus in a good many ways, by the time we reach our early teens, the figure of Jesus himself has ceased to be credible to us and to a large extent he has become an unreal person. To all this there is added yet another obstacle in the way of our understanding the person of Jesus. It is that, until quite recently, most books about Jesus and his ministry that used biblical quotations were all in an English that is not our own. That was of no particular importance in days when people in school were accustomed to reading Shakespeare as part of their ordinary English curriculum from a very early age, but such is no longer the case. When our formal worship, our hymns, are also often cast in an archaic English, we are subtly given the impression that Jesus, his life, his work, and the things he is reported to have said, are in some way or other a kind of fairy tale—perhaps of a rather superior kind, but nevertheless a fairy tale—which we would for many reasons like to think was true, but which with some reluctance we have come to regard rather skeptically.

This book is, as I have said, an attempt to produce a life of Jesus. It is written in the hope that it will provide you with material for discussion or further investigation. I hope you may be able to appreciate Jesus as a flesh and blood person, and as someone whose life and work is vitally concerned with what you do, think, and say, in this latter part of the twentieth century.

background

background

1. coming in the flesh

One thing about which we have to be very careful is that the Christian faith is about God and not about the life of Jesus. There is no possible excuse for any of us, however young we may be, not being careful and precise and as exact as we can be in our thinking about the Christian faith. Theology is about God, and theology is a science, with its own disciplines, its own ways, its own methods, of arriving at what may be known about God. Our difficulty is that so much of the language we use in hymns and in prayers is very often the language of poetry and not the language of precise theological thinking. It is therefore important, as we think about the life of Jesus, as we think about what he did, and what he said, and who he was, that we shall be as precise as possible. There is no point in your attempting to discover what the Christian faith is, and at the same time trying to express it by means of sloppy expressions or words which are not as exact as they can be. After all, there is a precise language about baseball and football; there is a precise language about the construction of an automobile or the way in which a space craft takes off from Cape Kennedy. If, therefore, we are to use the most exact language we can to describe anything that is of consuming importance, we have no right to go around using inexact language to describe the Christian faith (which we are told is the most important thing in our lives). In talking about the life and ministry of Jesus we have a duty to get our words, our vocabulary straight.

The Christian faith is about God and not about Jesus particularly. We talk, for instance, about God as Holy Trinity, Father, Son and Holy Spirit. Yet we so easily fall into the trap of supposing that Jesus or the ministry of Jesus is really all that matters about the Christian faith. Nothing could be more untrue. To understand that, we must now go back a little to things that are not in the strictest sense part of the life of Jesus. We must begin with the Bible, including the Old Testament, because the Bible contains the charter and foundation documents of our faith. Nothing will excuse a Christian not understanding what the Old Testament is about.

Our faith says that God deliberately chose to make himself known to men, particularly and especially through one people, the Hebrews, who were later called the Israelites, and by the time of Jesus were called (and are stilled called) Jews. Though the Old Testament goes on to say that God showed himself to the Hebrews and allowed himself and his will to be understood more fully through them than through anyone else, we believe he showed himself once and for all in the Messiah, Jesus. Here let us be careful. The Old Testament does not say, the Christian faith does not say, that God did not allow himself to be known or understood by other people apart from the Hebrews, the Israelites, the Jews. St. Paul, in the first part of a letter he wrote to people in Rome[1] is very insistent that people could always get to know a good deal about God through the ordinary processes of nature and through the way in which people themselves behaved. St. Paul is here going back to the Old Testament idea that God in some way or other made man as the summit, or the pinnacle of his creation—made man, as the Bible says, in his own image.[2] Nevertheless, it is the case that the Old Testament, the New Testament, and our Christian faith, all say that God declared himself, showed himself, and allowed his will to be understood, far more fully and completely through the Hebrew history than through anything else. It was one of the more memorable remarks of Pope Pius XII some years ago, that we are all spiritually Hebrews. He was not trying to say more than St. Paul says in his letters, but it is a condition of which occasionally we need to be reminded. Our inheritance as Christians is bound up with Judaism, with the whole history of the people of Israel, which Christians believe reached its climax in God's revelation of himself in Jesus.

Two thoughts may help us just a little to understand what is meant when it is said that God showed himself more particularly and especially to the Jews.

First, it is not necessary to know very much about the gods of antiquity, whether in Egypt, in Greece or in Rome, to realize that in the end no educated sensible thinking person could believe in them for very long. The Greek and Roman gods were only too human; they were far too small. They were just like you and me, warts and all. The Egyptian gods may have been slightly more believable but even they were probably far too much concerned with the agonies of men. The Egyptian religion was mostly bound up with the idea of "pie in the sky"—almost anything goes here on earth, so long as you get rewarded in heaven for your agony.

Second, we must remember the continued existence of the Jew not only as a factor in our own history here in the United States, but as a factor all over the world. There is no other single people which has been more conscious of its identity as a people than the Jews have been. They have persisted through torture, death, persecution, exile, defeat, and disaster on the pages of world history for almost four thousand years, and they are still with us, highly self-conscious as a people. Somehow or other if we decide that we can wipe out altogether the idea that God showed himself especially and particularly to the Jews, we must explain the continued existence of the Jew as a self-conscious unity to our own day. So then, we have here an important thing with which to reckon.

It is impossible to grasp the Christian faith unless you have first seized hold of the idea (which is part of our faith) that God many, many centuries ago chose out one particular people through whom he would make himself known to men, one particular people through whom he would in the end show himself finally to men. Without this kind of understanding, nothing that we can do to understand Jesus, nothing that we think about him, will be of much use. He must be seen against a background of his own people, against the background of his own birth, against the background of his tradition. His tradition was the tradition of the Jew.

One more thing: Not only does the Old Testament say, not only does the Christian faith say, that God showed himself and his will particularly to a special people, but it also goes on to say that God bound that people, the Hebrews, the Israelites, to himself by a "covenant."[3] That word should not need any explanation here, as long as it is understood that in this context "covenant" does not mean a "mutual assistance pact" between God and the Hebrews. It was not that God would come inevitably to the rescue of his people, whether they were good or bad, just because there was a covenant between them. It was not that God was always bound to defend his own. The word "covenant" essentially means that God bound the Hebrews, Israel, to himself to be his own people, his own absolute possession.

Whatever excuse some other peoples might have for not knowing God, or not knowing God's will, the burden of the covenant was this: The Hebrews had no such excuse at all. Always they were bound to God, to the one true God. For Israel there could never be any excuse for idolatry; there could never be any excuse for peering over the shoulder and wondering whether, after all, the gods of other peoples might have something to be said for them. That, incidentally, was a very great temptation to the Israelites when they came out of the desert and began to settle in the agricultural plains of Canaan, the country later called Palestine. They often *did* look over their shoulders and ask whether after all the Canaanites, the people who lived on the land and who knew the ways of agriculture, might have something to be said for the gods they worshipped.[4] But the prophets always insisted that however bad the circumstances might be at any particular time, the Hebrew, the Israelite, never had any excuse. He was always bound by the covenant which God had made with them.

Later on, to the original idea of covenant, there was added yet another idea—that of a "royal" covenant under David. It was understood as meaning that in some sense the kingdom of David, the throne of David, would go on forever. The idea of the kingdom of David, the royal house of David, the covenant of the kingdom, a sense that God would somehow always uphold that kingdom and covenant, exercised an extremely powerful hold on the imagination of all Jews from the time of David onwards. Indeed when we get to the time of Jesus it was probably far more alive than it had been for some centuries, and when we come to talk about the ministry of Jesus we shall see just how powerful the idea was.

Footnotes: [1] Romans 1:18 to end.   [2] Genesis 1:26.   [3] Exodus 19, 20.   [4] Judges 2:11–23.

2. birth

To begin where most things begin, that is to say, at the beginning, we shall discuss briefly the birth of Jesus and the circumstances which surrounded him as a small child. Here we must start with something purely negative, by getting rid of whatever impressions remain in our minds from things like Nativity pageants, Christmas stories repeated for us in carols, and the kind of pictorial illustrations with which most of us are familiar.

We do not know the precise date of Jesus' birth. The choice of December 25 was dictated not by any knowledge of the time of year at which Jesus was born, but because long after the life and ministry of Jesus, the Christian Church chose a pagan Roman festival, the Feast of the Saturnalia on December 25, so that Christians could have a legitimate reason for celebrating a

holiday along with their pagan neighbors. There were other reasons that dictated the choice of December 25. By looking up in
an encyclopedia and discovering what the Feast of Saturn on
December 25 was about, you may get some hints or clues as to
why early Christians decided that that was an appropriate birth-
day celebration for Jesus.

Not only do we not know the precise date of Jesus' birth in
the sense of month and day, we do not know the year in which
Jesus was born. As for this, there has been a good deal of controversy in years past, and in fact the controversy still goes on. The
birth of Jesus is agreed by most scholars to have taken place between the years 9 and 6 B.C. If this strikes you as a little strange
(that we should be talking of the birth of Jesus in years B.C., that
is, "before Christ"), this is not quite as odd as it sounds. For one
thing, in spite of the apparently very precise notes of date and
time given in the gospels of St. Luke[1] and St. Matthew,[2] there is
a considerable amount of difficulty in sorting out who took
office, and when, in the Roman province called Syria of which
Palestine was, at that time, part. Almost our only firm dates are
the dates of the reign of Herod the Great (37 to 4 B.C.), and the
taking office as prefect of Pontius Pilate in A.D. 26 or 27. Even
here some flexibility remains. Also, you will know from your ordinary studies in school, the calendar has been subjected to
change several times in the centuries following the ministry of
Jesus. The last great change, an astronomical recalculation, took
place during the pontificate of Pope Julius in the 16th century,
and this has led consequently to a good deal of confusion in the
Christian mind as to what constitutes B.C., "before Christ," and
A.D., "the year of our lord."

We must begin with John, the cousin of Jesus. His mother
and Mary, the mother of Jesus, were cousins. You will remember
from St. Luke's account that John the Baptizer (or Baptist), as
he was later called, was born to Elizabeth and Zechariah in their
old age—an unexpected birth and announced by what we are
told by St. Luke was an angel.[3] Let me remind you that all
through the Bible, wherever angels are said to have appeared on

earth, they have been mistaken at first for men. Do let us try to get right out of our heads the perfectly dreadful pictures produced in the nineteenth century of angels as rather drooping females wearing somewhat oversized nightdresses and with wings of goose-feathers. If you must think of angels as something other than men, if you want a picture in your minds of what angels are like, then please remember that for the majority of the writers of the Bible, angels were God's warriors and God's messengers.[4] Messengers and warriors have no business to be made to look stupid. John the Baptizer then was born six months before Jesus. It is significant that when Luke tells us that the parents of John were old when he was born, he also tells us that when John was a youngster, he was "in the desert until the day when he showed himself publicly to his people." [5]

"In the desert" we now know to be almost a technical term, often used to describe the Essene community at Qumran, which will be discussed in a later chapter. The supposition of many New Testament scholars is that John the Baptizer, the cousin of Jesus, was sent as a small boy (probably when his parents died) to the Essene community at Qumran to be brought up along with other similarly orphaned children. If that is correct, then it was from the Essenes that John gained his great insights into what the coming of God's kingdom might mean. It would also seem that John came to the conclusion that the kingdom of God was much nearer than the Essenes believed, and so left them on that account. Of John's birth then and of his early years, we know very little. He comes to us in the pages of the gospels as a full-grown man and an ascetic, who spent many years mulling over in his mind when and how God would redeem his promise to visit his people. Incidentally, it was a Jewish scholar, Paul Winter, who some years ago proved that the three songs which appear in the nativity stories of John and Jesus in St. Luke's gospel and which are still sung in some churches—the Benedictus,[6] the Magnificat,[7] and the Nunc dimittis[8]—are three very old hymns which probably dated back to the days of the Maccabean wars in the second century B.C.

We must now turn to the birth of Jesus. It seems almost a los-ing battle to try to inject some kind of common sense or histori-cal perspective into the kind of thing that is said, or acted, about the birth of Jesus in Nativity plays or Nativity pageants. If you want to read or even at some time to act Nativity stories or pag-eants, either go back to the Middle Ages to what were called "mystery plays" or, for something approaching an up-to-date ver-sion of the Nativity story, read "The Man Born to be King" by Dorothy Sayers.[9] Far too much damage has been done in times past by a habit (which owes more to the sentimentality of adults than to the desire of children themselves) of producing Nativity plays and pageants at Christmas time. There is no need to detail that kind of thing, but it is hard to imagine any reason for mak-ing the gospel a fairy tale by dressing up improbable angels in paper wings.

The birth of Jesus was announced to a young girl, probably fifteen or sixteen years old, called Mary, or in Hebrew "Mir-iam," who was engaged to a man older than herself (who may have been a widower) called Joseph. Once more, let us take note that when the angel appeared to Mary, she mistook him for a man, a perfectly ordinary human being. She was very perturbed at the news that she was to bear a child, particularly when (as she went on to say) she was engaged to Joseph and certainly had had no sexual relations with her future husband or any other man. It is important here to remember that in Jewish law at that time, two people who were engaged were as good as married, and the marriage ceremony itself was a seal or sign of a contract already made. Mary's consternation therefore is easily understandable. She was told by the angel that her child would be conceived through the direct agency of God.[10]

Let us get straight here what is meant when Christians talk about the Virgin Birth or when our creeds talk about Jesus being born of the Virgin Mary. What is being said by the Christian documents is that the part of Jesus' life which in ordinary cir-cumstances he would have received from a human father, he re-ceived directly from God. Now, if it could be proved decisively once and for all that Jesus was born through the perfectly ordinary biological processes through which all of us were born, this would not destroy the Christian faith. If, that is to say, it was ever proved decisively that Jesus was born by ordinary sexual generation, this would not destroy what the Christian faith says about him. The Christian faith says that in Jesus, God spoke definitively to all men, and that Jesus was God in human flesh. God could accomplish this through the perfectly ordinary means, just as easily as by what Christians call the Virgin Birth. Without laboring this point over much, you will want to think over one more thing in connection with the Virgin Birth: Whenever men have talked or thought about God walking this earth in human guise, they have always tended to suppose that when or if God did this, he would intervene in human affairs by some very special means. The idea of a Virgin Birth is certainly nothing new when we come to the pages of the New Testament—as an idea, it is scattered all over the literatures of ancient people. So the question to which you should direct your minds is this: How and why did men get the idea that when God came, or *a* god came to visit men, he would do so through an out-of-the-ordinary means? As a matter of fact, you might care to put some of your own ideas down on paper. Why did men get the idea that when or if God ever came among men, he would be born in a very special way of a mother who had never had dealings with an earthly father? There are very important questions here, but we will not go into them.

Understandably, Joseph was very considerably upset when he discovered that Mary was pregnant. This was a scandalous state of affairs because he knew perfectly well that he had had no sexual relations with his future wife. He therefore determined, being a compassionate man, but at the same time wanting to uphold the Law of Moses, that he would quietly divorce Mary. Our New Testament sources tell us that he was warned in a dream not to do so and that he was told who the future child would be. He would be the Deliverer of the people of Joseph and Mary.[11] What the New Testament means when it talks to us of dreams or of visions, we do not know. We can be matter-of-fact and suppose that Mary discussed the matter with her future husband and explained as well as she might the interview which had taken place between her and her visitor. Joseph at any rate maintained the engagement, and we must presume that they were married before the birth of Jesus, or shortly afterwards.

It was at this time that a taxation census was put out in Palestine, the details of which are now completely lost to us. Apparently each person had to go back to his own city to establish his identity and his family background. It is said that Joseph was of the lineage, the family of David. There is nothing in the least bit improbable in this, for Jews were extremely careful about matters like genealogy and tribal lists; and plainly, David, the second king of Israel, who had reigned a thousand years earlier, would by that time have had a very considerable number of descendants. Joseph and Mary, therefore, set out to go to Bethlehem.[12] It was a small city, probably no more than five hundred people at this time, and you know the story about their finding no room in the town's hostelry.

We must avoid here any suggestion of callousness or hardheartedness on the part of the keeper of the inn. Our English in some versions says "there was no room for them in the inn." It would be far better if the translation read "there was no *place* for them in the inn." The innkeeper was doing his best to preserve in the difficult circumstances of the registration and census the ritual law concerning child-birth. It was not only that in the open courtyard of the inn there would be no privacy for the birth of the child, there was also the consideration that in the crowded circumstances of that inner courtyard there would be many who inadvertantly would be involved in the ritual "unclean-ness" of childbirth.[13] This would pose a considerable number of problems for the innkeeper who would have been responsible for the whole thing. He was therefore doing his best not only to preserve some degree of privacy for the mother and her unborn child and for Joseph, but also to make certain that the provisions of the law with regard to ritual unclean-ness were being observed.

Bethlehem then as now, had many caves underneath its dwellings, where animals and stores were kept. In one of them, the innkeeper lodged Mary and Joseph. It was while they were in Bethlehem that Jesus was born.[14] St. Luke does his best to give us a dramatic picture of the birth of Jesus. The apparent poverty of the birth, or at least the poverty of the circumstances (though it is worth remembering that the innkeeper was doing his best) contrasted with the promises God had made to his people—contrasted with the destiny of the child who had been born, and Luke paints for us a picture of angels appearing to shepherds in the outlying hills, telling them of the birth of a Deliverer.[15] As we shall see, the country was then ruled by Herod, who was considered a foreigner and who was, in turn, subservient to the Roman Emperor. There would be nothing particularly surprising at that time in the history of Palestine of groups of people getting the idea that the Messiah, the promised Deliverer, had indeed been born. Talk of the kingdom of God was very much in the air, and there had been a good many people who had claimed to be precisely that—the promised Messiah, the promised Deliverer.

I want now to turn our attention for a moment or two to the husband of Mary, to Joseph. For many centuries we have been misled by a fourth century report that Joseph was a carpenter.[16] Probably you have seen pictures, most of them very bad, of the boy Jesus helping Joseph in a rather curiously nineteenth-century carpenter's shop. The first person to suggest that Joseph was a carpenter was a Bishop of Caesarea, named Eusebius. It is possible that when he made his statement, he was relying merely on one facet of the translation of an important Greek word. The Greek word which is used to describe Joseph in our New Testament is the word *techtōn*. If you take off the last syllable *ōn*, and put *arch* and then *i* in front of what you have left, you have "architect." This is important; *techtōn* in Greek certainly does not mean "carpenter" though it may include some of the things that a carpenter does. Quite certainly the word means "a craftsman" and a craftsman of a fairly high order. We are not justified in supposing that Joseph was a kind of village carpenter, hacking out plowshares, or making the odd door. A certain amount of research in the Smithsonian Institution in Washington will convince you that the merest peasant can make a plow. He may experience some difficulty in fitting an iron tongue into the plow, but as the early settlers in America discovered, it was possible in the absence of the proper instruments to make a workable plow, to be drawn by an ox or a mule, out of the forked branch of a tree. We are therefore being remarkably stupid if we attribute to Joseph the status of a mere village carpenter. The word "craftsman" is a much better translation, and it suggests a man in a fair way of business who traveled around the country quite a bit. Possibly it is from this traveling of Joseph's from one place to another that we owe the suggestion in the gospels, not only that he was living in Nazareth and had to travel some eighty-five miles to Bethlehem to register for taxation, but also that he found it not at all difficult, when rumors began to reach King Herod that an important child had been born, to take Mary and the child to Egypt. When Jesus later on spoke quite sharply of his own poverty,[17] and called his immediate followers to join in it, his poverty was voluntarily chosen, he came from a family background that was at any rate reasonably comfortable.

So Jesus was born in Bethlehem, which is in Judaea, in the southern part of Palestine. It is, as you know, only about five miles from Jerusalem, and we must remember that Palestine was a crossroads of trade routes and people were accustomed to moving about a great deal, either on foot, or by donkey and mule. Too often we picture the first-century Palestinian as hardly traveling at all, bound to a life of toil, and hardly ever moving outside the confines of his own little community. Jesus' birth undoubtedly prompted a good deal of speculation among those few who knew something of its inner circumstances, or guessed that there were unexplained features about it.

We now have to turn our attention to a group of people who are depicted for us in the second chapter of St. Matthew's Gospel as coming to see this child from a distance.[18] First, if you look up the passage in the New English Bible, you will find that the people who came to see Jesus are described as "astrologers," and not by the more familiar phrase, "Wise Men," which we know from the King James version of the Bible. This is very important for our understanding of what this episode means. Once again, if you put onto the end of *magi* the syllable *cian*, you will get "magician," and *magi* of course is part of "magic." The magician is a dabbler in magic, sometimes a slick operator in magic. Second, these people who came to see Jesus, are certainly not described as three in number; still less does St. Matthew give us their names. Third, we have no business whatever in the interests of historical truth to go around singing little Christmas carols, inventing "Kings" just because they happen to please us.

What is said about these astrologers is that on seeing some astrological signs in the skies, they came to Jerusalem. There, they set some officials in the city by their ears by demanding to know where the new Messiah, the new King had been born. Herod the Great was not a Jew, but a native of the neighboring enemy country, Idumaea, the Edom of the Old Testament; he had married into the old royal Hasmonean (Maccabean) family and had, through intrigue and with the backing of the Roman Emperor, usurped the throne of Judaea. All his life Herod lived in fear of some traitor, some claimant to the throne, some Jew left over from the Hasmonean dynasty, who would dethrone him and reign in his place. At different times he had executed his second wife, Mariamne, several members of her family, and several of his sons because he suspected them of just such plots against him. Herod's reaction to the astrologers' news can be readily imagined. In the story, the astrologers, having discovered from people who had made a study of such things in the Hebrew scriptures that the new Messiah might be expected to be born in the city of David, Bethlehem, went there, found Mary and Joseph, gave to the infant gold, incense, and myrrh, and did him honor and reverence. Then, having been warned in a dream what Herod was about, they went back to their own place another way. So far, the story is fairly simple, and on the surface of it, quite straightforward. But it is when we look at this word "Magi" to describe these visitors more carefully, that we begin to realize there is just a little more to the story than meets the eye.

The astrologer in the time of Jesus was a figure of fear. Enormous wealth accumulated in the hands of men who claimed to be able to read the signs of men's destiny in the stars. By and large, it was a very superstitious age, and Jews were not wholly immune from it. (Josephus, the Jewish historian, speaks of astrological symbols in the Temple.) It is worth recording that Julius Caesar, the hard-boiled Roman soldier, found it quite impossible to conduct a military campaign without an attendant astrologer, who could read the signs in the skies, and the omens in the entrails of a slaughtered chicken. Astrology was a serious business. It was big business. If you went to consult an astrologer on any problem whatsoever, you could be reasonably certain that the interview would take place in a darkened room, filled with clouds of smoke produced by a mixture of incense and myrrh. You could also expect that you would be charged an extremely hefty fee for the privilege. So now please let us notice that these people who are reported to have come to see Jesus gave to him gold, myrrh and incense. In other words they are presented as giving to Jesus the tools of their trade and the gain that they collected from it.

Did the visit ever take place? It is impossible at this remove to know exactly what the truth of the matter might be, but the earliest Christians who commented on this passage in St. Matthew's Gospel appear to have thought that Matthew was in fact telling a story not necessarily true, but with a moral attached to it. It is as though Matthew is saying, "When the Lord of all things was born, when the Messiah came to his people, when God appeared in human flesh, magic and the old superstitions knew their day

was up." Interestingly enough, the Greek of the story will carry
the translation that the visitors to Jesus did not "present him
with gifts," but "gave up their loot." That is a perfectly legitimate translation of the Greek. We need to try to put ourselves
in the position of someone who first heard or first read the story.
To have said at that time that magic was dead, that its empire
had come to an end, was a tremendous claim. To claim that it
came to an end with the birth of a child in an obscure Judaean
town was an even more tremendous claim. Whether therefore
this story of the visit of the astrologers, these high priests of su-
perstition, is historically true or not, it at any rate contains for us
and for everybody the most important assertion of all—that
when God comes, everything that stands in his way must give up
and stand to one side.

Moreover, Herod's reputation for slaughter and bloodshed,
impressive though it was, has left no record of any bloodshed or
slaughter in Bethlehem or around it. It is difficult to imagine
that Herod could have executed a number of people, a number
of small children in Bethlehem, the city of David, without inviting some kind of attention, but our principal Jewish historian,
Josephus, knows nothing of it—or if he does, never mentions it.
What does seem to be historically accurate is the report that Joseph and Mary took Jesus away into Egypt, where they stayed
for some considerable time until Herod was dead.[19]

Footnotes: [1] Luke 3:1-2. [2] Matthew 1:1-17, 19-22. [3] Luke 1:5-25, 39-
79. [4] For example, Psalms 34:7; Exodus 23:23; Revelation 12:7-12. [5] Luke 1:
80. [6] Luke 1:68-79. [7] Luke 1:46-55. [8] Luke 2:29-32. [9] New York: Harper,
1943. [10] Luke 1:26-38. [11] Matthew 1:18-25. [12] Luke 2:1-5. [13] See Leviticus
12:2; 15:19-23. [14] Luke 2:6-7. [15] Luke 2:8-20. [16] Matthew 13:55 is the basis
for it. [17] Matthew 8:20. [18] Matthew 2:1-12. [19] Matthew 2:13-23.

3. family and childhood

So it was that when the little family returned (as we are told
by Matthew), Joseph and Mary elected not to go into Judaea,

but went to where Herod's influence was more limited—north to Nazareth.[1]

It is here that we reach one of the most baffling things about the life of Jesus. Why do we know nothing of his early years? How did he grow up? What did he learn? What sort of games did he play? At what sort of age did he begin to realize that he had a particular destiny marked out for him? We have to rid our minds of any idea that the gospels are biography. It is worth remembering that biography is a relatively modern discipline, and though lives of people were not unknown in the time of Jesus, they were nevertheless not the kind of painstaking and exact biography that we expect now when we pick up the life of a prominent man and endeavor to see what makes him tick. The people who wrote our gospels were not writing biography. They were concerned with one thing, and one thing only—that God in Jesus had visited his people, that God in Jesus had given to man a completely new beginning, that everything before the teachings and ministry of Jesus was simply preparation. A good deal of biography could therefore be left out altogether even if it was known. Furthermore the picture of Mary the mother of Jesus as she comes to us from the New Testament is that of a retiring girl and woman, not seeking the limelight, always on the outskirts of what her son was doing and saying, and it is only when we get to the period of the very early Church in the Acts of the Apostles that she comes fleetingly into our view again.[2] Therefore, if you are looking for precise biography in the life of Jesus, you will be very disappointed.

This is the best place in which to deal with one matter which from time to time causes some bewilderment—the matter of the family of Jesus. One thing is clear to begin with: by the time Jesus began his ministry in Galilee he had been away from the scenes of his childhood so long that people did not recognize him. And it is their questioning which prompts the mention of Jesus' "brothers and sisters" (Matthew 13:53 to end; compare with Mark 6:3-6). Jesus himself is told that his mother and "brothers" are waiting to see him (Matthew 12:47; compare with Mark 3:32 and Luke 8:19), which prompts him to compare the disciple who listens to him as being as close to him as his own family. We gather from John 7:3 that there was active hostility towards Jesus on the part of some members of his family, though St. Paul later on tells of "James, the Lord's brother," being head of the church in Jerusalem. Who were all these people? Judging by the kind of things which are indicated to us in the gospels, they were all older than Jesus. Perhaps the most sensible suggestion is that they were the children of Joseph by a former marriage. When we say the Creed at the Eucharist, our faith (and the gospel records) demand that we give our assent to the belief that the mother of Jesus was a virgin when Jesus was born. The Creed does not state that she remained a virgin, and indeed many Christians read the plain words of Matthew 1:25 as ruling out the possibility that Mary and Joseph never had sexual relations. Roman Catholic and Eastern Orthodox Christians, however, maintain that Mary remained a virgin all her life. Our understanding of all this is made a good deal more confused by the suggestions, which began to be made some centuries after the time of Jesus, that Joseph himself never had sexual relations with anyone at all. On this view, the "brothers and sisters" of Jesus were actually cousins or some other kind of family relationship. It is true that the terms "brother" and "sister" can often be applied very loosely, in both Greek and Hebrew, to people who are not related to the speaker, and this was the explanation which St. Jerome favored (the same Jerome who translated the Hebrew and Greek scriptures into Latin in the fourth century). Orthodox Catholic theology, expressed in the creeds and councils, has maintained (from the New Testament) that Jesus was conceived of a virgin mother.

There is only one story in Scripture between the birth of Jesus and his emergence upon the field of Israel's history (probably in his late twenties)—the story of his visit to the temple with Mary and Joseph when he was a boy of 12.[3] We have to assume that the upbringing of Jesus was as normal as that of any other Jewish

boy of his time. He was circumcised and given his name
("Yeshua") when he was eight days old,[4] and by this act taken
into the covenant relationship which God had made with his
people, the Jews. If Joseph and Mary traveled around a good
deal in the furtherance of Joseph's work, as they probably did,
then undoubtedly Jesus would have accompanied them. He
would have been taught to read and to write from the Hebrew
scriptures, an exacting and painstaking discipline which is per-
petuated among orthodox and conservative Jews up to this time.
It is not in the least bit necessary to suppose that Jesus was an ignorant peasant. He would have learned his reading and writing
from the synagogue in his own town. After all, one of the principal functions of the synagogue was, and still is, to act as a school.
As to the journey to Jerusalem at the age of twelve, the age at
which most Jewish boys now celebrate their Bar Mitzvah (com-
ing-of-age, assuming the adult responsibilities of their faith), we
can say that there is nothing particularly surprising in the incident as it is recorded. Do let us beware of finding the miraculous
in the commonly accepted sense of the word, where there are
properly speaking no miracles to be found.

Jesus remains behind in Jerusalem, evidently enthusiastic and
entranced by everything that he sees. After all, Bethlehem,
Nazareth, and Capernaum were tiny places, unimpressive com-
pared with the glories of city and temple in Jerusalem. He remains behind, sits on the fringe of people who are listening to
teachers expounding the Hebrew scriptures and expounding the
Law. Jesus, sharply perceptive, asks questions and everyone is as-
tonished. Joseph and Mary go searching for him, and when he
meets them they are evidently travel-worn, not a little frightened
and bewildered by this child who confronts them with the question, "Didn't you know that my Father's house was the right
place to look for me?"

We must now turn to see what Jesus learned about himself.
This is an almost impossible task, but you should try to see the
growing up of Jesus through your own eyes, through your own
person, and through your own imagination. Those of us who

have had recent dealings with very small children, either in our own family, or the children of friends, will know that very small children for the first few years of their lives go through a series of exhortations: Do this, Do that, Don't do this, Don't do that. That is part of our ordinary education. We are now all of us sufficiently grown-up to have forgotten what those early days are like, because true self-consciousness does not begin to dawn until we are six, seven, or eight years old, whatever the age of self-awareness might be in the case of each one of us. We have to assume therefore that Jesus went through this process of growing as you and I did, with the same series of Do this, Do that, Don't do this, Don't do that, and that he went through the same kind of warnings when he went out to play: not to go too far away, to come when called, to be where he was wanted to be at the time he was wanted. But what is much more startling for us is the assertion of our faith that Jesus was without sin. And I want us if possible to try to understand what this means. I have spoken of self-awareness, self-consciousness. At what stage in your life and mine did we, thinking over in our childish minds how many times we had been told Don't do this, Don't do that, wonder what would happen if we *did* it, whatever it was? What I am asking you to imagine is Jesus going through the same process that you and I went through in our very earliest growing years, and being faced with exactly the same questions with which you and I are faced: "What will happen if I do this?" Inevitably, in the life of each one of us, there comes a moment when, knowing all the prohibitions that have gone before, we choose to try out what is merely *suspected* to be forbidden. I am saying as simply as I can that Jesus grew up as any other boy of his time grew up. But I am also saying that we have to see Jesus facing this first crisis of his self-conscious life, this first facing of the question, "What will happen if I do this or that?" and deliberately turning his back upon the temptation to disobedience. That is what we mean when we speak of Jesus as being "without sin," and I think when we are young, it is the most difficult idea of all for us to understand. We are so accustomed to the idea of disobedience to God's will, disobedience (hidden or open) to parents and others, as a part of human life, that we find it extremely difficult to suppose that God ever meant it any other way. But the Christian faith says that God did not mean it that way. And if we wish to see man as God meant him to be, then we must see man *in Jesus*. Somehow, having the idea that sin, disobedience, is part and parcel of our lives, we try to shy away from the idea of the sinless Jesus, but there is nothing particularly weak or spineless about obedience—it is the hardest lesson we ever have to learn. It is all the harder when we are young, because very often there is little or no time to ask for reasons for some particular course of action being forbidden to us. Often, too, we are aware of many things that we would like to do as to which nothing has ever been said to us by way of Yes or No, and yet we are at the same time aware that what we are proposing to do may be wrong. Any adult who has anything like a memory at all will be only too aware of the painful struggles which all this can bring upon us in childhood. So the giving of his life in total obedience to God was not something that came more easily to Jesus than it does to you and me.

When we are very young, perhaps up to the age of eleven or twelve or so, we are on the whole far too busy about our own concerns, far too busy about the kind of excitement which life itself can provide, to be troubled about precisely *who* we are. But it is when this period of childhood begins to pass over into adolescence and youth that questions about our own real self, our own real identity, questions about what it means to be a person, start coming to the surface. Who am I? What am I? What am I going to be? What will I be like in ten, twenty years time? How much have I learned? How much more is there to learn? At exactly the same time in our lives that we are becoming aware of what it means to be a *self*, a *person*, the body in which that *person* lives begins its own headlong rush into adolescence, youth, manhood and womanhood. There is certainly nothing that we can do to stop the process once it is started, or even to slow it down, or hurry it along, but it is a period of acute crisis in the growing youngster's life, and you are being asked to put yourself in imagination in Jesus' place. He too, at adolescence, began to face the same crisis of identity. Who am I? What have I learned? How much more is there to learn? What does it mean to be a *person?* What does it mean to be a man?

We have already emphasized that Jesus brought to this time of his life a whole childhood which had been given in total simplicity to God. And this total giving to God made the crisis, the pain, and the uncertainty of his adolescence and youth all the more heart-searching, all the more in need of an answer. There is reason to suppose that Jesus may well have spent the latter years of his childhood in the desert community with the Essenes at Qumran (we will discuss this later). He will have had ample opportunity in the solitudes of his own mind and in the physical solitude of the desert to face the question of identity. It is therefore at least possible so far as we can judge that it was at the end of his childhood and the beginning of his adolescence that Jesus began to discover his own proper place, his own proper vocation. There is, of course, the very real possibility that his mother may already have told him something of the special circumstances of his birth. We may suppose too that if he and his cousin John the Baptizer were at Qumran together, they may well have not only studied together, learned their lessons together, but also have had ample opportunity to speak with each other of the fortunes of their own people and the hope that God had provided for them, that he would one day provide his own deliverer.

Jesus then, stands on the edge of manhood, just as you and I are standing, or have stood, on the threshold of one kind of life, as we bid goodbye to another one which is behind. Of these years of Jesus' adolescence and youth we know nothing at all. It is no use wishing that we had information about those days, for as we know, the gospels were not written to provide you and me with interesting biographies of interesting people.

Footnotes: [1] Matthew 2:22–23. [2] Acts 1:12–14. [3] Luke 2:41–51. [4] Luke 2:21.

4. first-century palestine

The immediate background of Jesus' life and ministry can be studied in two parts. The first part will be fairly short; the second is going to call for a good deal of explanation. Here then is the first part:

Once again you must do your own work over this because it concerns geography. Palestine always occupied an extremely important place in the ancient world. If you look at the map of the Mediterranean, especially a physical map that shows fertile areas and desert, you will see how this was so. Palestine occupied a central place on the north-south trade routes between Egypt and Syria. It had a coastal plain which was very fertile, where most things grew, where the climate was equable, and where a good many people settled. There was constant travel all through antiquity through Palestine. This, incidentally, is of considerable importance when you come to talk and think about the ministry of Jesus. We are very often, I think, given to suppose that until someone invented bicycles or automobiles or railroads, no one traveled at all. In fact, people were given to doing a great deal of walking over ground you and I probably wouldn't choose to walk on except deliberately and as exercise. Travel was constant. In low-lying areas there were fertile plains with water, and the uplands (increasingly so as one climbed higher away from the sea) were more like the high desert of Oregon or Nevada than anywhere else that you are likely to see. The uplands would support sheep and goats and (given a certain amount of irrigation) olives and figs. These lands were very dry, very hot; beyond them, up in the hills and the mountains, is what in the Bible is known as the "wilderness" or the "desert." Once more one can appeal to the mountainous parts of the American desert. The Jordan valley, which runs from north to south and spills eventually into the Dead Sea, is almost tropical in the north, very light in vegetation. As it descends to below sea level, it runs through desert and is intensely hot. Very few people can bear living anywhere near it and indeed, in antiquity, no one did live alongside the lower reaches of the Jordan valley. I warned you I would say little about the geography of Palestine, but it is important for the kinds of separation which it made between various kinds of people who inhabited Palestine in the time of Jesus and before him.

Here then is part two. By the time of the birth of Jesus, the three hundred-odd years after the return of the Jews from exile had been marked by very bitter fighting, both with Greeks and with neighbors, and also by the splitting of the Jews themselves into multitudes of sects and divisions. Not by any means the majority of Jews had elected to come back from Babylon. Many of them had spread all over the Mediterranean world and had displayed an aptitude for both trade and banking. And in Syria-Palestine itself, the picture was anything but that of a unified people.

At the time of Jesus' birth, Palestine was, along with Syria, a Roman province, under a prefect appointed by the Senate in Rome. It was true that the Jews had a king, King Herod, who began to reign in the year 40 B.C. Herod was almost uniformly hated by all the Jews because he was not a Jew himself. He was by birth from the country of Edom, and the Edomites had been bitter enemies of the Jews ever since the invasion under Joshua centuries before. Herod is depicted very often as cruel, ending his life as almost insane, a man given to harboring suspicions about his family, his successive wives, and almost anyone who had dealings with him. It is, perhaps, an unrelieved picture of gloom. Nevertheless it is worth bearing in mind that Herod took his job sufficiently seriously to spend a great deal of his own money in founding places of learning and also in combatting anti-Semitism wherever it was to be found. He was also extremely successful in putting down brigands and robbers all through Syria-Palestine, and not for centuries after his death was the country ever as safe again. It is therefore important for us to bear in mind as we read the New Testament records that there were other sides to Herod's character. He was certainly cruel, certainly suspicious, and at the end of his life probably mad.

As for Judaism itself, the culture into which Jesus was born, it was torn by internal strife—party strife, we would probably call it. But since many of the groups in question find their way into the pages of the New Testament under their own names, it is necessary that we spend a little time over them so that they will not be too difficult to remember when we come to them.

First, then, the Pharisees. We are not very sure of the meaning of the word *Pharisee*. It can in fact mean one of two things, *Persianizer* or *separatist*. The meaning *Persianizer* has been suggested by the fact that the Pharisees were intensely interested, as a religious group, in things like angels of light and angels of darkness, things like the final warfare at the end of time, when there would be one tremendous cataclysm between the forces of good and the forces of evil. They were probably indebted for this interest to ideas they had picked up from the Persians and woven into existing Hebrew thought. At the same time, this doesn't quite explain how these people, if they were so attracted by foreign ideas, could have been so fiercely patriotic. For Pharisees, if they were nothing else, were intense and dedicated patriots. It is for this reason that most scholars have thought that the word Pharisee actually means *separatist*. Among Jews, the Pharisees were conspicuous for their determination to uphold the ideal of Jewish separateness from all other peoples, an ideal that had developed during the Babylonian exile, five centuries before the birth of Jesus.

The one distinction that made the Jews separate, marked off from all other people, was of course their possession of the Law or, as they generally called it, the Law of Moses, recorded in what are now the first five books of our Old Testament. The Pharisees saw that if the Jewish people were to survive, they had to be marked off and separate from the rest of the peoples around them. There had been, as a matter of fact, a long drawn out battle of wills during the time of the Greek invasion of Palestine. A good many Jews had been attracted to the Greek theater, to the Greek gymnasium and sports, and a good many Jews found themselves so fascinated by Greek culture and Greek literature that they had, according to some Pharisees, given up all claim and title rightly to be called Jews at all. The Pharisees would have none of it. They were determined that, whatever else happened, Judaism would be separate. At the time of Jesus, therefore, the Pharisee emerges not only as a super-patriot but also (and this we would find hard to discover from the pages of the New Testament) a representative of the party of the ordinary common people. Whatever else the ordinary common people in the time of Jesus may or may not have had, one thing that many possessed was a burning patriotism and a desire to throw off the yoke of the Roman occupying authority.

If you like, you can draw parallels between first-century Palestine and the thirteen American colonies before 1776. It may help you a little to understand why these Pharisees, who were so rigidly dedicated to the details of the law, should have found themselves a party of the common people.

The other party of which we hear a good deal in the New Testament is that called the Sadducees. Here the name is much more easily explained. It comes from Zadok, the name of the chief priest under King Solomon, and the Sadducees included most of the Jerusalem temple clergy and many of the clergy who lived in the environs of Jerusalem. Not *all* of them, it is true, but *most* of them were Sadducees in the sense that not only did they claim descent from the priests who had anointed Solomon as king over Israel in the 10th century before Jesus,[1] but also because they declared that they would have nothing to do with the newfangled theological ideas of the Pharisees. No angels, no final warfare between good and evil, no sort of speculation as to where good and evil came from, and, above everything else, the Sadducees maintained that only the law of Moses, only the first five books of our Old Testament were to be held as scripture at all. The Pharisees were perfectly willing to admit into the public reading in the synagogue the books of the prophets, for instance. Not so the Sadducees. The Pharisees could maintain that there had been a constant belief all through Israel's life in resurrection. The Sadducees replied that there was no explicit mention of resurrection from the dead in the first five books of Moses and hence it was not legitimate for a Jew to talk about resurrection. At the same time, Sadducees found themselves, as temple clergy, in the rather odd position of being sort of civil servants for the Roman occupying power.

Not only were they responsible for the conduct of all temple sacrifices and all temple ceremonies, from which they derived a good deal of income, but they were also effectively in control of some civil services, including money exchange, the teaching of the young in the ritual law, and the administration of the affairs of the capital. By most common people they were regarded as snobs. They were regarded by ordinary folk with all the contempt which sometimes you may have heard adults use for the bureaucrats. In fact, they were bureaucrats; they were civil servants; they were often men of great wealth. That being the case, they were not likely to look with favor on the idea of anyone upsetting the *status quo* in Palestine by revolution. The Pharisees talked, hoped and prayed, and thought about "change." The Sadducees, whatever else they may have thought, would have none of it. They wished to maintain things just as they were.

You read in the New Testament of another group of people, the Scribes. The word, of course, means a writer, but it is used in the New Testament in a rather special sense. The Scribes were by and large not as well educated as the Pharisees, but they did have a facility for making note of the sort of decision which lawyers made (and the Pharisees were laywers) and writing them down. This exercised a tremendous influence on all Jews in the time of Jesus. The extent to which the Law, and the Pharisees' interpretation of it, influenced daily life can be understood best by looking at a specific example. It was forbidden for any Jew ever to walk over the grave of a person who had died. Now obviously, a good many people had died in the course of centuries in Palestine. How were you to know whether, when you were walking over your fields (if you were a farmer), you had or had not walked over the grave of someone or other? Of course, you couldn't be sure. Certainly you wouldn't go on digging forever, just to make sure nobody was buried under your land. What the Pharisee would say, and the Scribe would diligently write down, was that you should "purify" yourself at the end of the day by bathing. After all, the body of a dead person was in some sense rather mysterious; it had a certain kind of what the Jew called "holiness"—a certain quality of untouchableness—attached to it. Very well. Supposing in the course of your scraping the ground with your rather primitive plough, or looking after your sheep, you did take seriously the Pharisee's decision which the Scribe had written down. Water was precious in the uplands, and (as anyone will tell you who has ever lived in the desert) the winds are very hot and can really do great damage to the skin, so one of the things you do *not* do is bathe frequently. In this case the Pharisee's decision would condemn the peasant to a hard choice between wasting precious water and living in a perpetual state of ritual uncleanness. According to another law, insects that crawled were forbidden food, forbidden material for the Jew to eat. Indeed, in some senses they were treated as almost as "untouchable" as a dead body, in much the same way that some of us react to the more repulsive bugs—like the cockroach. But of course a peasant farmer was always coming across bugs of one kind or another. What was he to do? The Pharisee would tell him to bathe two or three times a day in order to keep his ritual purity. Just as we often resent the bureaucrat who enforces an unpopular law, rather than the legislator who is really responsible for it, people resented the Scribes, who wrote down and preserved all the leisured Pharisees' decisions that created extra burdens for the ordinary peasant farmer. At the same time, while the Scribe was regarded as a great nuisance, the Pharisee (for all that it was he who was actually making this kind of legal decision) could get away with it because he was a patriot.

You will find that the Anchor Bible commentary on St. Matthew's gospel has consistently translated one Greek word—which is rendered in our English Bibles as "hypocrite"—by such terms as "pettifogging lawyers" or "shysters" (especially in Matthew 23, where Jesus criticizes the Pharisees and Scribes). This has been done deliberately. For far too long we have allowed ourselves to think that the Greek word "hupocritēs" meant someone who was acting a part, whose real convictions didn't match the kind of public statements which he made or, worse still, whose public stands on various issues were not matched by his own conduct. But the Greek word, both in classical Greek and in the Greek of the New Testament, means someone who is "*hyper*critical" and overconcerned for the minutiae of the law. It is grossly unfair to the Pharisees, both in the time of Jesus and subsequently, to lump them all together as "play-actors" or some such perjorative term. Jesus' real criticism is that the Pharisees—and the Scribes—by their pettifogging attention to minute details of legal interpretation had reduced the Law of Moses from a liberating, joyous service of God to a very real burden.

We know that the lines of demarcation between various interests in Judaism in the time of Jesus constantly crossed and recrossed, and it is not easy to make hard and fast boundary lines. But there were recognizable features or patterns common to the groups which we have mentioned, and Paul made very good use of one such distinction, of which you can read in Acts 23:6–11.

One further party among the Jews ought to be mentioned here. We do not know with anything like certainty when the Zealots arose as a distinct group within Judaism. The Jewish historian Josephus thought that they arose when the Roman authorities conducted a census in A.D. 6 as a direct basis for taxation. This humiliation of subjugation to a foreign power was felt by Judas the Galileean and Sadduk the Pharisee to be more than they could bear, and they led a revolt against Rome. Some modern scholars have dated the origin of the Zealots as a distinct sect to about A.D. 66, but that appears to be far too late. We know that at least one of Jesus' disciples was a Zealot—or was nicknamed such (Luke 6:15; see also Acts 1:13). In some Bible translations the same man is called "the Canaanite" in Mark 3:18 and Matthew 10:4, but that is just a transliteration of the Aramaic word for Zealot. Some scholars have thought that Judas the traitor was also a Zealot, and this idea gained some ground because his name, Iscariot, could be derived from the Latin *sicarius* (dagger), thus naming Judas a "dagger-man." But it is far more likely that his name derives from the place-name, *Kerioth*. What is certain is that the disciples of Jesus must often have heard discussed in Galilee the fate of those who had resisted the Roman incursions, and must often have heard talk of further resistance.

Footnote: [1] 1 Kings 1:39.

5. essenes and samaritans

We shall now turn, for the sake of the early years of John the Baptizer, and of Jesus himself, to yet another group of people, about whom we have discovered a tremendous amount since 1947, a group of people about whom we now know almost as much as we do about any other group within Judaism. They are the Essenes, and unfortunately no scholar has ever come up with any convincing explanation of what that word means. We come across the name all over the place in ancient authors, particularly in the Roman historian, Pliny, a highly cultivated and highly educated man, and also in the eminent Jewish historian, Josephus; both of them used the word Essene, or Essenes, as though everyone knew exactly what it meant. Unhappily for us, we do not know what the word means at all. We do know, however, a great deal about how these people thought and a great deal about the way they behaved. As I have indicated, they were extremely important, not only for the early years of John the Baptizer and the early years of Jesus, but also because of their influence on early Christian thought as it appears in the New Testament.

One of the things which has given us a great deal of interest in the Essenes has been the discovery of a very large body of the writings produced in their "schools," a collection of writings which are commonly called the Dead Sea Scrolls. The first of them came to light in 1947, at a time when scholars had little hope of discovering any fresh material that would throw light on the background of Jesus and the New Testament. It will be necessary here to say something about the origins of the Essenes, and I hope that as this account of the life of Jesus goes on, you may discover for yourselves the links which many scholars think existed between Jesus, his disciples, and the early Christians, on the one hand, and the Essene movement, on the other.

The movement began between the years 160 and 140 B.C. in response to the devastation that had been caused by the Greek invasions of Syria, Palestine, and Egypt and the attempts by the Greeks to force their own culture on the Jews. The Essenes emerged from that background as totally separatist and very patriotic; therefore they appealed to the Pharisees at a later date. The Essene movement was originally founded by a figure who is known to us only as the Right Guide and who, after twenty years of trying to find some location in which his followers might settle, finally decided upon Damascus. It was there, after his death round about 135 B.C., that his followers compiled a kind of "confession of faith," which our scholars call the Damascus Document, the Code of the Covenant, or sometimes the Zadokite Document. The Essenes were bitterly opposed to the Jerusalem priesthood, because after independence was achieved, the Maccabean princes who had led the revolt against the Greeks, and who had eventually usurped the high priesthood to themselves, had turned out to be no better than other secular rulers. The Essenes, fiercely dedicated as they were to Israel, to the Law, and to the Covenant, looked with determination to what they called

the end of the age, when after a final cataclysm of warfare between the forces of good and evil, God would usher in his final
kingdom. They were composed of a broad cross-section of Jewish society, both priests and laymen, with an inner council of
twelve. They held that official Judaism, centered in Jerusalem,
had deserted the Covenant. They regarded the Temple and its
priesthood as something to be totally rejected. For them, the
idea of the Kingdom of God was a tremendous driving force.
They looked for, and prayed for, the coming of the Age of the
Messiah. (Incidentally, I trust that you know that the word
Messiah means "the Anointed One," and referred originally to
the anointed king of Israel, and in later ages to a Deliverer
whom God would appoint to restore the fortunes of his people.)
The Essenes, however, looked not for one Messiah but for two,
the one belonging to the priesthood, who would be more or less
in final control of affairs, and the other a secular ruler called the
"Messiah of David." Many of the Essene writings explain at
great length the way in which God would restore Israel; there are
even battle plans in some of the documents for the final gathering of the forces of good against the forces of evil. One thing is
clear: In the restored fortunes of Israel, the Essenes regarded
themselves as the rightful heirs and inheritors of the destiny of
the Jewish people.

The Essenes have left us a good deal of information about
themselves. They were numerous, broadly representative of the
people, and geographically widespread. Many of them were perfectly ordinary married people, but there were also settlements
of Essenes gathered in what are best described as monastic communities. One such has been excavated at Qumran, near the
source of the Dead Sea. That community appears to have been
quite populous and its graveyard contains the remains of about
two thousand people. From the Essene literature we can gain a
very clear picture of the kind of life these monastic Essenes led.
There were very strict rules about entering the community; the
person who entered had to give up his property to the community; he could not marry; and of him there was required unques-

tioning loyalty and obedience. The area near Qumran had sufficient fresh water springs to grow dates and olives and even provide for the upkeep of sheep and goats. For a rather unpromising area, it is quite surprisingly fertile. The community had its own tanners, its own shepherds, its own millers, its own blacksmiths, its own schoolteachers, and indeed for most ordinary things, appears to have been quite reasonably self-supporting. Community life centered not only round a daily work load, which everyone was expected to share, but also a common meal. Whether in fact, rejecting the Temple as they did, the Essenes and their communities ever had any system of sacrifice such as obtained in the temple at Jerusalem, we do not know, but it begins to be clear from archeological investigation of the remains at Qumran, that they *may* have had a simple sacrificial system.

One thing is interesting for the light which it sheds on the mission of John the Baptist and on the practice of the early Church —the custom which obtained among the Essenes of "ritual washings." They were very particular about maintaining their ritual purity, in the manner of all Jews; but with the Essenes idea of ritual washing seems to have taken a further step, and it is ultimately from them that we derive our practice of baptism in the Christian church. The person who wished to become an Essene was required to undergo a washing as a sign that he had rejected his previous way of life, that he had repented of his former sins, and that he was now ready to embrace a totally new way of life. It is worth pointing out here that this is not the same thing as Christian baptism. Christian baptism claims to *do* something, whereas Essene washing or baptism was merely a sign that the man who came to it had already done what was required to be done. In technical theological language (which, as I have said, you should know and use), Christian baptism is an "effective" sign, whereas Essene baptism was a sign of something which had already been done, a seal upon its completion.

We know that large numbers of people came to the Essenes for a greater or a lesser period of time, to spend time among them, reading, studying, learning the Law, and generally learning Essene thought, and the Essene way of life. Among people who did so was the eminent Jewish historian, Josephus. We have referred earlier to the Essene practice of taking in young orphaned children to be brought up by the community. We know that there were a good many such, and in reference to the infancy of John, and possibly even Jesus himself, it may help you to understand one or two things which are said in the New Testament, almost as a side glance, or a thought by the way.

At the moment the most important thing for you to remember about the Essenes is their passionate dedication to the Law, to Israel, and to the idea of a future kingdom of God.

The next group of people to which we must refer is the Samaritans. We know a great deal about them from two later books of the Old Testament, Ezra and Nehemiah, and we know from the New Testament that Jesus had extensive dealings with Samaritans. After the resurrection of Jesus, the disciples undertook a fairly large-scale mission among the Samaritans as the very first piece of missionary enterprise.[1] The Samaritans were a mixed race. When the Jews centered in Jerusalem had been carried away into exile in the year 586 B.C.,[2] the Babylonians left behind in the country the poor peasantry, a few lesser people in the government, and even some of the lesser clergy. Unlike the Assyrians, the Babylonians did not make a practice of devastating a country which they occupied. Instead, they generally left behind the ordinary peasant farmers, so that the land should not become a desert. In process of time, the Jews so left behind married some settlers from other areas whom the Assyrians, the Babylonians and the Persians had brought into Palestine. Therefore by the time that numbers of Jews had begun to return from the exile, the Samaritans were a very mixed lot indeed. They did, however, consider themselves in all essentials Jews. They acknowledged only the first five books of our Old Testament and were, in this respect, like the later Sadducees. But the returning Jews were not in the least bit inclined to come to terms with Jews who had married and intermarried with surrounding peoples, and a great deal of bitterness attended the final separation of Jews and Samaritans, some three or four centuries before Jesus.[3]

The Samaritans were very conscious of their separation, and did their level best always to insist that they were descendants of Abraham, that their lot and their inheritance was essentially those of the Jews themselves. They tended to live almost for self-protection in a marked-out area of Palestine, round Mount Gerizin, maintaining their own way of life, their own priesthood, and their own sacrificial system. Incidentally, and of some importance, is the fact that the Samaritans themselves had no temple and (like the Essenes) totally rejected the Jerusalem Temple and its sacrifices in Jerusalem. Here we come to one rather interesting fact, and it will be of some importance to you in your reading of the New Testament if you can remember this little detail. It is this: At the time of Jesus, the Samaritans called themselves "Hebrews," which meant that neither the Essenes, nor the Jews in Jersualem, would touch the name "Hebrews" at all. Some scholars think that this explains the title to one of our New Testament books "to the Hebrews," and they think that that book was addressed to a group of Samaritans who had become Christians. So then the Samaritans called themselves, rather self-consciously, "Hebrews." The Essenes insisted that they were the "true Israel." The Essenes did not call themselves "Jews," they did not call themselves "Hebrews," they called themselves simply "Israel" or "the returned of Israel." The vast majority of Jews, with a sacrificial system centered in Jerusalem, referred to themselves as "Jews." So here you have three names for people whose racial origins, national origins and religious origins were pretty well the same—Jews, Hebrews, Israelites.

In any study of the New Testament, it is useful to understand something of the language patterns in Palestine. At the time of Jesus, for all ordinary purposes of trade, commerce, and travel, for purposes of communication between one people and another, the common language of the whole Mediterranean world was Greek. It could be educated Greek, it could be market-place Greek, but nevertheless, the one single language that bound together all the Mediterranean peoples in the time of Jesus was Greek. We very often look at a map of the Mediterranean in the time of Jesus and discover that all the Mediterranean world was Roman. If we are not careful, we shall assume that Latin was spoken all over that area. That would be completely untrue. Latin was the language of a comparatively small area. In Italy it was the language of the army; it was the language of the administration of the Roman law courts, at any rate so far as rendering verdicts and sentences was concerned. But Latin was essentially a language that belonged to the imperial authorities in Rome, and not to the provinces. It was commonly thought for many years that Aramaic (the old imperial language of Assyria and Babylon) was the language spoken by the majority of Jews. This we now know to be not quite true. In the time of Jesus, Aramaic was rapidly becoming a series of rather widely separated dialects, whereas Hebrew was becoming more and more a spoken language, and a deliberately cultivated language at that. What you should do therefore, is to get out of your minds the idea that in the time of Jesus, Hebrew was a dead language. On the contrary, it was very much alive.

How many languages did Jesus know? He would probably have a working acquaintance with Greek in order to travel as he did around Palestine. For all ordinary purposes of commerce, of trade and of dealing with other people, Greek, as I have said, was the language that bound all peoples together. It seems therefore highly probable that Jesus would be acquainted with, and could speak, Greek. There is some evidence from the recorded utterances of Jesus in the New Testament that he spoke Aramaic, and also Hebrew. This would not be very surprising. He would have learned his Old Testament in Hebrew, and Aramaic and Hebrew are allied languages, in much the same way that French and Spanish are both derivatives of a common parent language, Latin.

Footnotes: [1] Acts 8:4–25.   [2] 2 Chronicles 36; Jeremiah 39.   [3] Ecclesiasticus 50: 25–26; Ezra 9–10; Nehemiah 2:19 to end; 13:23 to end.

ministry

ministry

6. john the baptizer

John the Baptizer, appears on the scene with dramatic sud-
denness.[1] It is not easy to say how old John was when first he
came to the notice of his fellow countrymen on the banks of the
River Jordan, with his strange cry that God's kingdom, God's
reign, was almost at hand. It is possible to make the guess that
he was between twenty and twenty-five years of age. It was a dramatic appearance, for John came onto the banks of the River
Jordan clothed in the skins of animals, undoubtedly (like Elijah)
with face and arms and legs almost blackened by the ferocious
heat of the sun, with the lean, hard look of a man who has
fought with nature, and the look of a man, too, who has fought
with God and with his own mind and self-hood. His appearance
was startling because it had long ago been thought by most of
his fellow countrymen that the age of the prophet was over. No
one supposed that there would ever be a return of the days when
a man driven by God's Spirit appeared on the public scene with
a dramatic message to give. It had been taken for granted for a
long period of years that the Law and the Temple were all that
God in his mercy was going to allow the Jews to have. There
were, most people thought, no more really dramatic moments in
history yet to come.

It was true, as we have seen, that there were groups of Jews,
passionate nationalists, who longed above everything else for
some tremendous intervention on the part of their God that
would for ever destroy their national enemies, give them secu-

rity, and even give them sovereignty and rule over all the surrounding peoples. From time to time there had been self-pro-
claimed deliverers who had briefly appeared on the scene,
attracted bands of followers, and attempted nationalist uprisings. By and large the uprisings had been of very short duration
and very violent, and had been put down with great ferocity. No
doubt, many of those who heard of the appearance of John on
the banks of the River Jordan greeted the arrival of this new
preacher with one of two attitudes. On one hand some would be
completely sceptical, would wonder what would be the end of
yet another claimant for national honor with a following of
semi-outlaws. Others, on the other hand, would dearly wish,
hope, and pray for the coming of God's kingdom, but would
have been warned by all the lurid stories of the past about what
had happened to those who made such claims and preached
such dangerous doctrines.

In the end, we are told that men flocked to hear John. His
way of talking evidently gave men the impression that he was
something more than just another fanatic, something more than
just another nationalist who wanted to lead a popular revolt.
Certainly there is a good deal of the language of John the Baptizer in the gospels of St. Matthew, St. Mark, and St. Luke that
strikes our ears as being very stern indeed. But quite certainly it
is not easy to read those three gospels without at the same time
being aware that there was something far deeper about John:
when he spoke of the kingdom of God it is obvious that he
spoke of that which must change men's minds—change the di-
rection of their lives—rather than of a kingdom created by the
sword. It is in the fourth of our gospels, St. John's, that we get
the most interesting of all the insights into John the Baptizer.
People came to him from Jerusalem, asking questions. The questions are almost breathless: Are you the Messiah? Are you the
expected prophet? Are you the One who was to come? And
John's reply to all those questions is: "I am not." John sees his
mission only as that of a voice, and if we think of this long
enough we can, I think, approach the figure of John the Baptist

with a great deal more wonder, and a great deal more reverence, than we commonly give him. "I am not." And when he speaks of the Coming One (which was a title for the Messiah) he says he is not fit to stoop down and loose the sandals off the feet of the One who would usher in God's reign.

To all of this John added something else. I have described before a little of what baptism meant in John's own life, and in the life of those with whom he was brought up. John gave to the old ritual washing an entirely new meaning. It became a looking forward to the day when God's reign will be declared to men. He did not say, as Christians do, that baptism was an entrance into a new life, a new relationship with God. He only claimed for his baptism that it *prepared* men for a new life of repentence, or as St. Mark tells us in his gospel, it *looked forward* to the forgiveness of sin. It has often been said by scholars (and there seems to be no real reason to doubt it) that John's ritual of baptism may well have been something that could be repeated often. That is to say, people who listened to John and his message may well have come back to him to be baptized more than once. John's appearance, as I have said, was dramatic, and even in our rather bad English translation we can sense something of the excitement which greeted the arrival of the strange new prophet on the banks of the River Jordan.

Then came the day when Jesus himself came to John.[2] St. Matthew's gospel provides us with an interesting scene between John and his cousin. John, the man who is content to say "I am not," to describe himself as being simply a voice, finds himself confronted with his cousin whom he has come to believe is God's appointed Deliverer; what is more, he is being asked to baptize him. John shrinks from it, according to St. Matthew, and says, "If there is one of us who needs to be baptized it is I, not you." The reply of Jesus in St. Matthew's gospel is easily understood by the technical Greek or Hebrew scholar, but does not succeed in coming across at all well in our English. Perhaps the best I can do is to say something like this: Jesus replies to John, "It is absolutely necessary for the sake of what is to follow, that I should represent all the people of Israel in obedience to God's demand." If you want to put it another way, Jesus is saying "God has given you a vocation, a calling, a responsibility, to preach repentence, and to ask that people be baptized, as a sign that they accept what you have said. How, therefore, can I stand outside the demand of God, which is spoken through you?"

All our gospels agree that the baptism of Jesus marked a very decisive point in his life. He was perhaps in his late twenties, emerging so far as we know into public life for the first time. Our gospel stories try to indicate the drama of the occasion, both for Jesus and for John, in terms of a vision of God's Spirit descending upon Jesus; so our gospels say "like a dove," with a voice that declared "This is my Son, the Chosen One, and on him my favor rests." It is very easy for us, if we are not careful, to read into this a great deal more than the writers of our gospels intended that we should read. They, after all, were writing for those who understood the technical language of their own time well enough. We, who live two thousand years from such technical language, are apt to fall into all kinds of traps. The dove was very often used as a symbol for God's people, Israel. So too, the word "son" is used in the Old Testament to describe not only the king, but also the whole people of God. Jesus therefore at his baptism sees his identification with his own people, with Israel, with the Jews, as something total and complete. But the realization that his identification is total and complete marks yet another stage in his own self-understanding, another stage in his growth to identity. He must at all costs be alone to face out the meaning of what has happened.

Footnotes: [1] Matthew 3:1–13; Mark 1:1–8; Luke 3:1–20; John 1:6–28.   [2] Matthew 3:13–17; Mark 1:8–11; Luke 3:21–22; John 1:29–34.

7. preparation for ministry

Mark's gospel uses a very dramatic phrase to describe the next stage in Jesus' public life. He was, says Mark, "*driven* by the spirit into the desert."[1] We have already said there is reason to believe that "in the desert" was a technical term in the time of Jesus. We may therefore suppose, though of course there is no proof of it, that Jesus went back for a period of time to the community which had given shelter, education, learning, and a sense of vocation both to him and to his cousin John—back, that is to say, to the desert community at Qumran. He was there, according to the gospels, for forty days and forty nights. This is, in Biblical language, a convenient term for saying "a considerable time." We have no means of knowing precisely how long this retreat of Jesus after his baptism lasted. He had now to face the consequences of the decisions he had made. He had accepted a total identification with his own people. He had come to see that it was part of his life, part of his ministry not only to be identified totally with his people in complete obedience to God, but also in a very real sense to see himself as being the summing up of his people, their representative in a single, special sense. That is not too easy for those who are brought up in a republic with an elected President to understand, but it was not at all a difficult matter for the Jew to see his own people summed up, or if you like, "encapsulated" in the figure of a King or a Deliverer. Just for the record at this point, it is easy enough for a subject of the British Crown to regard himself or herself as being summed up in, and represented by, the person of the Sovereign. (In the United States the one central thing which sums up and represents in a very special sense all the citizens of this country might be the Constitution.) Jesus then must face what is meant by his own acceptance of the idea that he sums up and represents the chosen people of God, and it is in the light of this that you and I must see the story of his temptations.

Here again we are very often dismally served by hymns, pictures, and books about the temptations of Jesus. Nowadays such romantic descriptions are quite inexcusable, since enough has been written on the temptations of Jesus by scholars to have made silly mistakes quite unnecessary. Once more I call to your attention the fact that our gospels are written with a particular people in mind and are written in what are best described as "headlines." In other words, you and I, if we were living in the days of the Apostle Paul, would have been able to fill in a great many of the details for ourselves, details which the gospels do not even bother to mention. When, therefore, Jesus is shown to us in the temptation story as being confronted by Satan, the Tempter, he replies in the words of three quotations from the Old Testament. These quotations are extremely important. Remember for purposes of what we are about to study that Jesus regarded himself not simply as *a* man, but as representing the *whole* chosen people of God. It is this—his understanding of the vocation that he is now facing—that is the subject of his very sharp temptation to reject this identification with his people and also to reject the idea that somehow in his own person he must live through all the story of Israel's pilgrimage to God. It is not surprising that the quotations in St. Matthew's Gospel, Chapter 4, which Jesus uses, are quotations which come from the story of the escape of the Hebrews from Egypt.[2] It was in their long desert wanderings of perhaps two generations that they had to face a crisis of identity as to their own future, their particular relationship with God, and their relationship with the peoples around them. It is those temptations which belonged to Israel's past that Jesus here faces in the solitudes of the desert.

The first temptation is quite simply *not* that Jesus is being tempted after fasting, simply to make a pig of himself and eat without restraint. What is here being suggested to Jesus is the same thing that, we read in the Old Testament, suggested itself to the Hebrews as they came out of Egypt. Why not, for the sake of our very existence, come to terms with all the people among whom we shall have to live? Why not adopt their ways? Why do we have to make a sharp distinction between ourselves and the rest of men?

"Man cannot live by bread alone" had been God's word to the Hebrews as they came out of the desert after escaping from Egypt. There are other factors to be taken into account besides those of earning a living. It was a constant temptation to the infant Hebrew people—Israel—in those days to make some accommodation with the peoples among whom they were to live;

there was constant temptation to forget, or to overlook here and there for the sake of peace, that they were a distinctive people with a very particular vocation. So Jesus, living again in his own person the acute temptations of his own people, living again the spiritual experience of Israel, was tempted to make his own mission one that would be more easily understood. He was being tempted to appeal to great masses of people by a popular "messianic" approach. That might even have secured for him adherents from outside Israel from among people dissatisfied with, and chafing under, Roman rule. He rejected the temptation by an appeal to God's word to Israel in a similar situation long centuries before. "Man cannot live on bread alone"—on the cold calculations of secular politics. Israel, man, he himself as Representative Man and Representative Israel, must always respond to the demanding word of God.

The second temptation is again compromise, but compromise of a very particular kind and character. Jesus sees himself (as his own people had seen themselves long before in their coming out of Egypt) as one upon whom God's very special favor and love had rested. Wasn't it possible, therefore, if God had specially chosen the people of Israel, that they could go their own way quite happily relying on the fact of God's choosing them, believing that God would always, whatever they did, in the end support them and defend them? That was always a very serious temptation right through the history of God's ancient people and the attitude is supported here with a quotation from scripture.[3] Here, as their representative, Jesus faces that very sharp and fierce temptation. It is one that we face, too. We believe as Christians that we are living parts of "the body of Christ," a phrase that is used in Church and is taken from St. Paul. Isn't it therefore the case that, whatever we do, however bad or however good, God is bound to look after his own? Isn't it the case that God is always bound to take us back? We can, so to speak, play the fool with God.

Jesus rejects this temptation by quoting again from the story of the Hebrews coming out of Egypt. Whatever else you do, you must not put God to the test. You must not suppose that God will always, in all circumstances, defend you and be bound to take you back. God is master, not you.

In the third temptation, again represented to us by means of a kind of picture of standing on a mountain and looking over vast distances, the temptation comes to him to compromise with the lordship and the sovereignty of God. You will remember that in the picture story Satan says to Jesus, "If only you will acknowledge that a good deal of all this that you see really belongs to me, then I won't do anything further to upset your ministry." If you wanted to put it another way around, it would go something like this: "If you will acknowledge that in the end there are a good many people whom you had better write off as hopeless, people you cannot change, then you will find that your ministry will be a great deal easier." Jesus replies once more in words which are taken from the story of Israel coming from Egypt. It is the Lord God whom you must worship, and no one else. There is here the picture of Jesus facing the terrible possibility that those whom he had every right to expect would receive his message, would either be completely indifferent or actively hostile. Was he therefore to ignore their hostility and minister only to those who would receive his message with gladness, or was he concerned with all the people of God? There are some lessons here, of course, for you and for me as Christians.

Footnotes: [1] Mark 1:12–13; see also: Matthew 4:1–11; Luke 4:1–13. [2] Jesus quotes three passages in answer to the three temptations: Deuteronomy 8:3; 6:16; 6:13. [3] Psalm 91:11–12.

8. disciples

Jesus, then, spent this time of solitude in the desert community working out the consequences of what he had seen to be his own vocation, his own identity and his own place among his own people. The consequences are not in the end simply concerned

with him as *a* man; they are concerned with him as the Man—
God's man. Jesus' next act on emerging from his retreat in the
solitude of the desert was to choose a band of people who not
only would be responsive to what he had to say, but also would
carry on the work which he had laid out before himself—carry
on the work, understand the message, and when his ministry was
over, be responsible for spreading the message of that work and
ministry.[1]

Here again it is necessary to read between the lines in our
Gospel story. We are too often apt to fall into the trap of supposing that Jesus called a number of men whom he had never
seen before and, by some kind of mysterious magic of personal-
ity, attracted them immediately so that they dropped everything
and followed him. That this is not true we can discover from the
first chapters of St. John's gospel.

Plainly those whom Jesus first called were men who had
known him and with whom probably he had talked at some
length on the banks of the River Jordan during the preaching of
John. What seems to have happened is something like this:
Peter, John, Andrew and James had gone back to their work in
Galilee. They went back to their work as fishermen, with plenty
of opportunity to think over, and talk over among themselves,
not only John's proclamation that the reign of God, the Kingdom of God was just around the corner, but also the cousin of
John, whom John had introduced to them and whom in all
probability they had seen submit to John's baptism. Jesus was,
therefore, not a total stranger to them when he came upon them
on the shores of the lake of Galilee. But it was one thing to have
listened to John, one thing to have taken note of the person
whom John had introduced to them; it was quite another thing
to take upon their own shoulders a decision that this man—this
man Jesus—was indeed the Deliverer whom God had promised.
Some of them were members of the Zealot Party, who, in spite
of all the recent history of bloodshed in following false messiahs,
might be calculated to take up the call of the kingdom with en-

thusiasm. But it is quite wrong to assume that those who first followed Jesus, this company of men whom he called round himself, were all of them simple and ignorant fishermen. They may have been simple in the sense of "single minded"—indicated in the hope and the prayer that God's kingdom and God's deliverer would come in their own lifetime. But to write them off as ignorant is something which, in the light of what we know about the education of Jewish boys at that time, is simply untrue.

It was not at all uncommon at that time for bands of men, varying in number, to attach themselves to a wandering teacher. (For purposes of gatherings on solemn occasions, such as Passover, this group would be regarded as a *Chaburah*, or familial assembly.) But the question which we must ask ourselves is how they supported themselves while they were in the company of their chosen teacher. After all, it was necessary for them to eat and sleep. It is possible that the father of James and John, whose name we know to have been Zebedee, was a fisherman of some standing and importance. We discover later on in the story that John was quite well known to a number of people in the house of the High Priest and was evidently able to secure entrance to that house quite easily. It may be that the economic circumstances of his family were quite comfortable. Again, later on in the story, we find Jesus able at least to rent a house in Capernaum—his poverty and the poverty of his followers consisted simply in that they had no certain dwelling place, no stake, so to speak, in any city or town where they lived temporarily.

How long the ministry of Jesus lasted is a matter of debate among scholars but it seems to have been not very much longer, at any rate in the *public* sense, than two years. And now as we turn to the teaching of Jesus it will be necessary for you to bear one or two things in mind.

The first of them I have mentioned several times already, and that is the "headline" character of the recorded words and acts of Jesus as they are in our Gospels. Those who wrote them had no idea that you and I, nearly two thousand years later, would be reading them in a country and language of which no one then had any knowledge.

Secondly, you can discover for yourselves (if you take the trouble to do it) that the recorded words of Jesus in all four Gospels can be read aloud in a little less than two hours. Obviously, Jesus had a good deal to say that was not recorded.

Thirdly, bearing in mind the headline character of our Gospel story, we are then left with a situation where we must pick our way very carefully indeed between what Jesus said publicly and what he said in private to his pupils—the disciples whom he had gathered round him. And it is upon this last point that I want to concentrate for a moment.

Matthew's gospel makes a very clear distinction between utterances that Jesus made in public and the private teaching given to the inner circle of his pupils. But the words Jesus addressed to his inner circle, and which were meant to apply to their circumstances, their calling and their ministry, are often repeated in books and in pulpits as though they were meant to apply to all men for all time wherever they might happen to be. That results in a very distorted picture. I therefore advise you when you are reading the New Testament, take very careful note of what Jesus said in public and the kind of instruction he gave which would apply only to his immediate pupils in the circumstances of his earthly ministry.

Footnote: [1] Matthew 4:18–22; 10:1–4; Mark 1:16–20; 3:14–19; Luke 5:1–11, 27–28; 6:13–16; John 1:35–51.

9. private teaching

An important part of Jesus' teaching is the great body of instruction which is generally, but mistakenly, called the "Sermon on the Mount." If you look at the beginning of the account in St. Matthew's gospel (chapter 5), you will see that Jesus sees a crowd coming to him, goes up a hillside apart from them, and there sits down and is joined by the disciples. In St. Matthew's gospel this long instruction, which is given to the disciples alone, to Jesus' inner circle, goes right through chapters 5, 6, and 7. The part of this great instruction which is generally called the "Sermon on the Mount" is addressed entirely to those who belonged to Jesus' inner circle of pupils and *not* addressed to the crowds. Jesus had quite other methods of teaching ordinary people.

The first part of this long instruction (Matthew 5:3–10) sets the stage for everything that is to follow. The word with which the Greek begins (usually translated in our English as "blessed" or "happy") is not easily translated at all. Perhaps the best word we can come up with is the word "fortunate." Jesus tells his inner circle of pupils that they are fortunate to be on the scene when God's reign, God's kingdom, is about to be openly declared.

It is worth spending a moment or two here to explain one or two of the words which come in this introduction. There are for instance, "the poor in spirit." That certainly doesn't mean poor-spirited or people who lack courage. It means people who know themselves for what they really are—helpless before God. "Those who mourn" are not to be taken as those who have recently lost relatives or friends in death. The meaning is rather that of people who sorrow for sin. And "those who hunger and thirst," who are hungry and thirsty for what our English calls "righteousness," are those who are longing for the day when God will defend, will vindicate, his rule and his reign among men. And finally the disciples are told that they must be merciful, that they must be single-minded, because only so will they see God.

But this little brief introduction ends on a rather solemn note. They are fortunate—they are to call themselves fortunate—when they are persecuted for the sake of God's kingdom. Then Jesus goes on to tell them what their function is in this reign, this rule, this Kingdom of God which is about to be inaugurated. They are to be the salt of the earth, the light of the world.

He goes on for almost the whole of this instruction to make quite clear to the disciples that the reign of God does not mean the end of the Law of Moses as they had learned it. On the contrary, the coming of God's Deliverer, the Messiah, means that the Law of Moses will be seen in its true light as an expression of God's will for men—that what is important is not the minute details of that Law, but the kindness, the mercy, the compassion of God, who gave that Law to his people. There is instruction about prayer; there is instruction about almsgiving; and there is a very solemn warning that it is not the place of the disciples to make a final judgment about who is or is not worthy to be included in God's Kingdom.

I am going to take the time here to say just a little about what we are accustomed to call the Lord's Prayer.[1] I want to do this for two reasons. First, I am personally convinced that we use it far too often, and its words have lost the meaning which they had for Jesus' first disciples. And second, I want to use this explanation as an opportunity to underline what I meant previously when I said that the Lord's Prayer, like almost everything else in the Gospels, is written in headlines.

So let us take the Lord's Prayer bit by bit and see what those words meant to the men who first heard the prayer as Jesus uttered it. Remember for what follows that those who heard Jesus use this prayer were Jews and would therefore find other words and other expressions suggested to them by the outline Jesus gave. "Father in Heaven." The word "Father" to a Jew suggested all the other titles that were used in the Old Testament to describe God's relations with Israel. God was described as Father, Husband, Lord of his people; and Israel itself was described as God's son, God's bride, God's servant. Incidentally, do not be misled by people who tell you that the title "Father" for God was something that Jesus himself first taught us. That is quite untrue. The title "Father" as a description for God's relation to Israel is quite common in the Old Testament.[2] "May your name be hallowed." For the Hebrew, a person's name was the person himself, so what is being said here is, "May you be held in reverence by us and by all men." Then, "Let the Kingdom come." It is extremely difficult for us to appreciate the intense urgency and longing with which Jews prayed for the coming of God's reign, for the coming of his promised Deliverer. But the sense of the prayer "Let the Kingdom come" is that even if that Kingdom does not come *through* us, then let it come even *in spite of* us. But let it come *now.* "Your will be done as in Heaven so on earth." "May your will be done in us, through us, even in spite of us, but let it be done."

The next little· piece of the Lord's Prayer reads rather strangely when it is translated into something like its original terms. It would read, "Give us bread enough for today and tomorrow." Why today and tomorrow? This prayer begins with a plea, a longing for the coming of God's kingdom, for the coming of the Messiah; and the petition, "Give us bread enough for today and tomorrow," indicates that the "tomorrow" which is spoken of is the great day of the Messiah's coming, in which men will not be able to work. The next petition follows on from it: "Forgive us sins, just as we, for our part, forgive sins and debts, for tomorrow is the day of the Messiah." Then finally, the petition for which we commonly use "and lead us not into temptation." The word "temptation" of course means "trial" and the original Greek and the Hebrew that are behind it can be translated something like this: "Do not let us be involved, caught up in, the birth pangs of the Messiah. But even if that must be, then deliver us from evil." It was a common belief in the time of Jesus that the coming of the Messiah would be heralded by distress on a large scale. The prayer asks that when the Messiah comes, God in his mercy will not involve this little community, this Messianic community of Jesus, in the distress and the pain and the anugish. And yet it goes on to pray that even if God does allow them to be caught up in the trials that are to accompany the coming of the Messiah, even so all will be well so long as God delivers them from all evil.

Now we must turn to the way in which Jesus taught the people who came to him. Remember we have already discussed the separation that we must make between private teaching given by Jesus to the inner circle of his disciples (teaching designed to prepare them for the future of the Messianic kingdom when Jesus was no longer with them), and the kind of teaching Jesus delivered to the public at large. Most of this teaching was done by means of parables. Here particularly we have to be very careful how we handle the material and how we understand the parables. The oldest parable we have in the Bible is in the second book of Samuel, chapter 12. It is the story which the prophet Nathan told to David in order to make a particular point and to get some kind of response from the king. What is important for us to notice here is not the story itself but what happened when Nathan got to the end of the story. In verse 5 of that chapter we read that David was very angry when the story was over. He said that the guilty person was worthy of the death sentence, but he would have to restore what had been stolen four times over, at the very least. Now the interesting thing about this is that David assumed that the story he had heard was a legal decision given to him as chief magistrate of the kingdom, delivered to him for judgment and for sentence.

[It was while I was engaged in preparing, with Prof. William F. Albright of Johns Hopkins University, a commentary on St. Matthew's gospel that we began to look at this whole question of parables all over again. We began with the example just quoted, relating to David and Nathan, and from there came to the quite firm conclusion that parable material (such as this) in the New Testament and in the period immediately following the New Testament in Jewish rabbinical writers was almost entirely legal material. That is to say, we were convinced at the end of our study that what we are dealing with in parables is a whole series of examples in "case law." This is a concept that ought to be familiar to both British and American readers, and when we had finished with the material in St. Matthew's gospel we were quite certain that it is the only adequate explanation for what we have come to call a "parable." As a matter of fact we were also led to some rather interesting conclusions about the prophets—who have left us many examples of parables in their writings. We came to the tentative conclusion that most, if not all, of the writing prophets were "covenant lawyers," concerned with the interpretation of the way of life of Israel under the law of the covenant.[3]]

Every now and again when a parable comes up in the ordinary course of reading the Bible, it is possible for us to get all kinds of meanings out of the parables which were not there originally *in the context in which they were first spoken*. For example, we are accustomed to reading or listening to the parable of the Returning Son,[4] sometimes called the Prodigal Son, as though it were simply a story about repentance. The point I want you to bear in mind is that that is not the original meaning of the parable as spoken by Jesus. The parables of Jesus made his listeners very angry indeed, so much so that a good many of them, seeing that the parables had a cutting edge that seemed to affect the listeners rather deeply, plotted to kill Jesus. So if the parable of the Prodigal Son was simply a story to persuade you and me that we had better come to terms with God, after wandering away from him by sin, then it is very hard to see why anyone should be very angry at it. Remember that Jesus addressed these parables to Jews, his own people, at a time when they were probably more keenly aware of their separation from other peoples than at any other time in their recent history. The parables are not stories told to encourage people to be good; you can do that in all sorts of ways. You can, after all, encourage people to be good by your own example. Sometimes you can encourage people to be good simply by batting them over the head and telling them to stop what they're doing. But Jesus' parables belong to a situation in which Jesus is proclaiming that in himself the very first signs of God's kingdom are already visible.

The parables pose one very sharp question to Jesus' hearers. The question may not sound very shattering to us today, but in the circumstances in which it was asked, it was enough to divide Jesus' hearers very sharply into several camps. The question was simply this: Precisely what do you make of your vocation, your calling, as God's chosen people with respect to those outside the community of Israel? In other words, what is your attitude when God's kingdom, the kingdom of the Messiah, dawns to the "Gentile"—the Greek, the Roman, the Arab? St. Paul spent a great deal of his time in his missionary journeys emphasizing over and over and over again that in the new Kingdom, in the Messiah's Kingdom, there were no distinctions of race. It was a battle he had to fight on a good many fronts.[5] For the Jew, the question was all-important. If Israel was God's chosen people, if Israel was the means through which God would show himself to the world, then wasn't it obvious that everyone who wished to have any part in this Kingdom must first become a Jew?

Footnotes: [1] Matthew 6:7–13; Luke 11:2–4.   [2] For example, Isaiah 9:6; Jeremiah 31:9.   [3] For example, Isaiah 5:1–7; 28:23 to end.   [4] Luke 15:11–32.   [5] For example, Acts 15:1–21; Galatians 2; Romans 11; Ephesians 2:11–22.

10. public teaching

So Jesus asked questions in his parables. Now let us have a look at one or two of them. Then you should be able to sort out the meanings of many of the rest of the parables for yourselves. Here then is the parable of the Prodigal Son, the son who wandered away from home.[1] There is no need to repeat the whole story, since you should know it very well. The outline of the story is simple enough, and identifying the central character, the father, is also easy. The father is God. But notice very carefully that the son who left home and said that he wanted to have no more to do with home or with his father (though at the same time claiming part of his father's goods) went away into a far country and wasted everything that he had obtained from his father. Then the story significantly goes on to say that the son finally managed to get a job looking after pigs, which only a Gentile could do. No Jew ever kept pigs. When at long last he came back to his father, he was, you remember, welcomed. But

notice the reaction of the elder of the two sons, and notice that
he *was* the elder. He complained to his father that he had never
left his father's side, that he had never wandered away, that he
had never wasted what his father gave to him, and back home
came the younger son, who had done all these things, and a tremendous fuss was made of him. So far, so good. The older son
who had never left home is the Jew. In constant touch with his
father, he was assumed to know the Father's will, and it was
taken for granted that he would always be at his Father's side.
But there comes the time when he, the elder son, must realize
that the Gentile, the non-Jew, is also a child of God. Try to
imagine the kind of reaction this story would have produced in
the minds of those who heard it. They were being asked to welcome into the kingdom of the Messiah those whom they had always regarded as hardly a people at all.

Another parable will help to set the record straight, and then
perhaps you might have a look at one or two others and see what
kind of an interpretation you can find for them. The other one I
want to look at now is the parable of the Good Samaritan.[2] It
has, as you know, provided us with the term "Good Samaritan"
to describe anyone who ever does a kindness or a service of great
compassion for someone else. That is a perfectly legitimate use
of the parable, and over the centuries a good many interpreta-
tions have been given to the parables that are perfectly right *in
themselves*, but that do not belong to the original meaning of
the parables as told by Jesus. Once more we need not go into the
details of the story itself. You know those well enough. Instead
we can concentrate on the characters in the story. There is the
man, battered and left half-dead by the roadside by bandits;
there is the priest who comes by and decides that he can do
nothing; there is the Levite who comes by and decides that he,
likewise, can do nothing. Last of all there comes the stranger, a
man from Samaria. Who is Jesus talking about when he dis-
cusses the man left for dead? He is talking about you and me,
battered, wounded, not by bandits, but by sin. Now if you had
been listening to this story as Jesus told it, you might have

grasped that particular meaning well enough to begin with, but you would have been in for a considerable shock when the next character introduced to you is a priest who decides he cannot help. The word "priest" to Jesus' hearers immediately suggested the temple in Jerusalem. It was only in the temple that sacrifices could be offered. It was never suggested that those animal sacrifices could take away sin, they could only look to the day when God would provide his own remedy for sin. The sacrifices were, in a very real sense, sacrifices of prayer and hope, that God would *hear* and forgive, although there was no certainty about that. Here then was Jesus saying quite flatly that the whole system of priesthood and sacrifice was helpless and hopeless to deal with men's real sickness, which was sin. Then the Levite: the Levite was likewise attached to the temple in Jerusalem, but Levites had a considerable number of functions; one of them was to act as a kind of choir, another to act as what we call servers, and another to be interpreters of the ceremonial law for people who came to the temple. You remember that the Levite looked at the wounded man and decided that he was none of his business. Jesus was saying that no amount of interpretation of the ceremonial law would do anything to remove the real sickness and the real damage of sin. Finally there came the stranger, the Samaritan. Samaritans were regarded with very considerable doubt, misgiving, and even in some cases, hatred by Jews in the time of Jesus. In any event, they were treated as outsiders, people who had, centuries before, compromised over the issue as to whether God's covenant and its promises were open to anyone except Jews. It was the Samaritan who bound up and took care of the wounds of the man left half-dead. But who is the Samaritan? The priest stands for sacrifice, the Levite stands for the whole legal system that surrounds sacrifice. That is easy enough; but the Samaritan, the outsider—where does he fit into the picture? The Samaritan is Jesus himself, the man from outside, the stranger, the person who has already excited a good deal of opposition because his interpretation of the kingdom is not the kind of thing that people really expected. And Jesus knew that ultimately (now that opposition was growing) he would find himself in peril of his life. And the Jew who was put to death, except in war, was regarded as entirely cut off from his own people. Jesus, even at this stage of his ministry, must have been aware of growing forces of opposition and hostility. Here he sees himself as The Outsider, bringing men wounded by sin, back home. So what are we to make of the final sentence in the parable itself, Jesus' reply to the man who had questioned him, and to whom Jesus had told the story? The last remark of Jesus, you remember, is "Go, and do the same yourself." Now that really does sound as though Jesus is telling us to be kind and compassionate and charitable to those in trouble. But we must search a little deeper than that. The true meaning of "Go—and as the wounded man received mercy, be merciful yourself" is: "It is only when you yourself know that in your time of need God came to your aid, that you will be in any kind of position to help anyone else. It is only when you and I know that we are powerless to do anything without God that we can really talk to anyone else about the needs of their minds and hearts."

If the whole point of the parable was simply to tell men to be good to each other, then there seems to be little reason for telling a story of such elaboration—after all, the Law contained more than enough material that told the devout Jew precisely how to treat his own brethren, and how to treat the stranger. Here we are being faced with a stern reminder that in order to *do* something rightly, we have to *be* something first. We cannot claim to bring men to God unless we know our own dependence on him. Only the man who knows his own desperate need of God can adequately deal with another man's similar need. This point was made with great force, incidentally, by St. Augustine (Bishop of Hippo, in north Africa, in the fifth century) when preaching on this parable.

Now we shall have a look at another example; it is to be found in the first part of chapter 16 of St. Luke's gospel. It is rather difficult to explain, and indeed up to fairly recently a good many scholars have disagreed considerably about what the parable means. In our terms it is about a wealthy landowner who discovered that his agent had been doing him out of some of the profits from his land. He sent for the agent and told him that he was being relieved of his job and would have to make an account of all his transactions. The agent was in rather a panic. He was not capable, he decided, of manual labor, nor did he wish to throw himself on the mercy of anyone else. So he called together people who were in debt to the landowner for whom he worked, and told them to take their bills and reduce the quantity of money which they owed to his boss—the idea being that when the agent was turned out of his job, those whom he had befriended in this way would feel indebted to him, and would find him something on which to live. In the story, Jesus says that the wealthy landowner congratulated his agent because he had acted rather smartly in looking after his own future. Then, Jesus goes on (in verse 9), "and so I tell you make yourselves friends of the unrighteous (or the unjust) Mammon, so that when *you* fail they will take you into eternal homes."

It has very often been said that the word "Mammon" means "money" so that what Jesus appears to say is that you had better make a friend of this awful thing called money so that when you find yourself on your uppers, somebody, somewhere, will have enough to take care of you. It never seems to have occurred to anyone that Jesus would never have been so wildly irresponsible as to describe money as "unjust" or "unrighteous." Of course money or property badly used *can* be, and often is, "unjust," "unrighteous," and (in the hands of the selfish) sinful. But it is not sinful in itself, and we must not suppose that what Jesus was doing here was to lump all property, and all money, together and call it evil. Mammon is an Aramaic word which our gospels put straight into Greek, but its precise meaning is not known.

So now we must begin to take this parable to pieces and look at the central characters again, even if it seems a little complicated at first. (There is no reason to be unintelligent about the

life of Jesus and certainly there is no reason to be afraid of looking behind the headlines into the real meanings of the words
and phrases of the New Testament.)

Very often in the New Testament, the Church, the Messianic
community which Jesus founded, is said to be the "Steward" of
God. Notice then in this parable there is a wealthy landowner,
who is God, and the steward, a land agent. If you want to put it
into modern terms, he is a real-estate dealer, acting for someone
with a great deal of property. Now, if in the New Testament the
Church is described as God's steward, then when Jesus is talking
about the steward in this story, he is describing his own people,
Israel, the Jews. They have been given insight about, and access
to, the will of God in a way that was true of no other people.
Jesus is here accusing them of misusing a sacred trust, and he
goes on to suggest that there is an accounting soon to be made.
What then, are his own people to do? The only thing for them
to do, when God's reign begins to expand into the Messianic
community (the Church), is to come to terms with those who
are heavily in debt to the wealthy landowner, the Gentiles. They
(the Gentiles) are heavily indebted to God for all the gifts of life
and creation itself. But in what way are the Jews to come to
terms? Notice that in the parable the land agent comes to terms
with his master's debtors by reducing their bills. I am quite certain that in this parable Jesus is asking his own people to face
the inevitable fact that when this little community of himself
and his disciples expands into that kingdom which we call the
Church, then very soon the Jew will find himself outnumbered.
Moreover he will be living in this community, in this church,
along with Gentiles who have never known the Law of Moses. Is
it fair to ask non-Jews to keep the dietary rules of the Law of
Moses? Is it right to ask Gentiles who have never heard of such
things to take particular care over ritual washings before eating,
cooking, sleeping, and so forth? Would it be fair to ask Gentiles,
for instance, to give up their practice of cremation after death?
So here Jesus is confronting his own people, who are coming to
him full of questions about this kingdom of God, facing them

with the inevitable fact that soon they must accept the fact that this kingdom which he proclaims will contain Gentiles as well as Jews.

It is in this light that you must look at the remark quoted earlier: "Make friends for yourselves of the unrighteous Mammon. Make friends for yourselves of those whom you have always regarded as sinners outside the Law, so that, when the time comes that this thing will have spread far beyond the borders of Israel, far beyond a little sect inside Judaism, they will take you as equals." This must have been an astonishingly hard thing to take, and Jesus goes on to say "If you cannot be faithful about this tremendous responsibility, then who is going to commit to you the true riches of God's kingdom?" This interpretation of the parable in St. Luke 16 is not the generally accepted one. Furthermore, there is no reference in Jewish literature following the time of Jesus to suggest that those outside Judaism were ever called "Mammon" or "the unrighteous Mammon." But to make the parable simply concerned with money makes very little sense, and in fact most of the scholars who write about it tend to say that there we may just be too far removed in time from the circumstances in which it was first spoken ever to be able to arrive at its true meaning. The interpretation here is given to you for what you may think it is worth.

The examples just cited should suggest that you look at parables with rather different eyes from those with which you may have regarded them previously. Most of the parables (in Matthew, particularly) are parables about the relationship of Jew and Gentile in the coming kingdom of God. If you can remember that, then with very little help you should be able to understand all the parables as they were understood by their original hearers. We are accustomed, of course, to use the parables in other ways. What we are concerned with in this life of Jesus is to put the parables back into their place in the ministry of Jesus, facing the same questions that Jesus and his inner circle of followers faced, in relationship to the challenge that Jesus' own ministry posed to his own people. After centuries of separation, centuries of self-consciously setting themselves apart from all the peoples around them, the Jews of Jesus' own time were so certain that the future belonged to them, that they hardly gave a thought to the idea that when the reign of God came among men, they themselves might be on an equal footing with all other men and not in a position of privilege. That was a question which, as you have seen, occupied a great deal of the time and energy of the apostle Paul in his ministry to Gentiles.

We have seen parables were used by Jesus, as they were by the prophets before him, as pieces of "case law" interpretation. There are other parables, particularly in St. Luke's gospel (for example, Luke 12:16–21) which are not directly concerned with the relationship of Jew and Gentile in the Messianic Community. But all the parables are presented by Jesus as "cases" for comment, and not simply as illustrations.

Now that you have a certain number of guidelines on which to work, you may try your own hand at interpreting a well-known parable—that of the great supper in St. Luke 14:16ff. One hint: the excuses which were given were not lame excuses, as you and I might think. They are perfectly valid reasons in the Law of Moses for excusing a man from military service (compare Deut. 20:5–9). Therefore ask yourselves these questions: Who is the host? Who was being invited? To what? (Remember that in the time of Jesus men thought that one of the signs of the age of the Messiah would be a great feast.) Who are the people who are invited in the place of the guests who would not come? Then you may pass to another great parable of a feast-day, St. Matthew 22:1ff. We are accustomed, quite rightly, to using these parables as warnings to us not to refuse God's call to us. What do you think Jesus was saying to his contemporaries in these parables?

We have spent some time over this because it is necessary for us to see the parables in the situation in which they were first uttered. Parables were as a matter of fact used by one very notable Rabbi (R. Akiba) shortly after the ministry of Jesus, but parables as such seem fairly soon to have dropped from view as a method of teaching. That was possibly because matters of interpretation of the Law become more and more a study of words. All this is not to say that the use that we make of parables in teaching and in preaching are wrong. Parables have demonstrated in Christian use and in Christian liturgy over the centuries a great flexibility of interpretation, and most of it has been quite legitimate inference from the words and the message of Jesus. Our only concern here is to attempt to place the parables firmly within the framework of the teaching ministry and teaching method of Jesus himself.

Footnotes: [1] Luke 15:11–32.   [2] Luke 10:29–37.

11. "signs"

Jesus' teaching in public may not have occupied such a large place in his ministry as we are often tempted to think it did. If you follow the indication given you earlier, and seek out for yourselves in reading the gospels how many times Jesus is said to have spoken to his disciples on the one hand, and to the crowds on the other, you may be rather surprised to discover how little public teaching there is in our gospels. Jesus traveled about a great deal, and St. John's gospel is mainly concerned with his traveling and teaching in the southern part of the country called Judaea, while Matthew, Mark, and Luke deal almost entirely with his teaching in the north, near the Sea of Galilee. It is almost impossible to work out a kind of timetable, but what *is* possible is to discover where the central point in all this teaching came. It is possible, that is, to discover from the gospels at what point Jesus could face his inner circle of disciples with the question "Who do you think I am?"

But before we come to that point, it is necessary to look at one other central feature of Jesus' ministry, that of miracles. In

any thinking that we do about miracles, there are one or two
cautions which have to be looked at before we go any further.
First, Jesus never spoke of his miracles as "proving" anything;
still less did Jesus ever suppose that people like you and me
might be tempted to speak of the wonderful things that he did
as though they *proved* he was God. Second, it is very necessary
to be cautious about what we mean when we think of miracles.
In spite of the fact that modern physical scientists are perfectly
well aware that there are vast areas of our universe that do not
behave in a regular pattern, the majority of people seem to think
that there is an ordered system of nature where everything goes
in a strictly ordered fashion, that can never be interrupted or is
never interrupted. To such people, the very idea of miracles, the
idea that the order of nature itself could be interrupted by something from outside, so to speak, is quite strange, if not impossible. In a very real sense, the physical scientist is entirely accustomed to what might be loosely described as "miracles." He is, I
mean, quite accustomed to the idea that the apparently orderly
pattern of this universe can very often break into all sorts of
strange directions for which there is no apparent explanation.
Third, it is only in Jesus that we can see man perfectly united
with and perfectly obedient to God. You and I have no idea at
all (except in Jesus) of what man, perfectly obedient to and perfectly united with God, is capable. Finally, almost everything de-
pends upon your own viewpoint. As recently as World War I,
aircraft were built of canvas, wood, and wire, and flew at about
ninety or a hundred miles an hour. Then, if you had told a
young child that he would live to see jet aircraft become com-
monplace, and to watch men land on the moon, using an instrument not yet invented (television), he would probably have regarded that as something either wildly impossible or, at least,
miraculous. Millions of children of that generation have lived
long enough to see the first moon landing and to understand it
as a natural, explainable event. There are all sorts of miracles
which surround us, day by day, and hour by hour, and very often
we don't even see them because we are not looking for them.

For my own part, I can hardly think of anything more miraculous than the whole mystery of birth itself.

It is very important to understand that Jesus did not use his signs of healing or of casting out devils as proving anything at all to do with himself. This is very important. Jesus, one gathers from the gospels, talked very little about himself. St. John's gospel has one particular word to describe these particular events of healing, or casting out devils; the word he uses is "sign." The miracles were signs of the coming reign of God; moreover, they were one of the ways in which that reign of God was shown to men. Perhaps I can best illustrate that by asking you to look at a dollar bill. The dollar bill has a two-fold function. It is not only a *sign* that the Federal Reserve Banks of the United States will guarantee you the sum of one dollar; the dollar bill is also the *means* by which the Federal Reserve Bank makes certain that you get that dollar. Or, if you want to put it another way, the dollar bill at first sight is a piece of paper, though, as a matter of fact, it is a highly ornamental piece of paper and not the kind of paper that one would use for writing purposes or simply for a bookmark. It is a special kind of paper, and it conveys a message and an importance that is all its own. In the same way the miracles of Jesus were not only *signs* that by these means the kingdom of God was coming to men, they were also the *way* in which that kingdom was coming to men in Jesus.

It is very important that we shall realize that nowhere does Jesus use the miracles as proof of anything about himself. He does not for instance say to us, "It is very important that you should pay attention to these miracles because they prove that I am God the Son." On the contrary, Jesus uses miracles as signs of his ministry, signs that God in him was bringing his reign very close to men. It is true that there are places in the New Testament outside the gospels where the miracles are almost treated as though they are proofs of who Jesus was.[1] But for the most part, there is very little appeal in the New Testament to the miracle stories as proving anything about Jesus himself.

St. John's gospel always refers to what we call miracles as

"signs" and perhaps for us that is the best word to use. If we want to find a convenient way of expressing what miracles are about, it is perhaps easiest to remember the phrase above: miracles are not only *signs* of the coming of God's reign to men, they are also the *means* by which that reign came.

It is also very important when considering these miracle stories not to be too clever. We may find in some of the miracle stories a rather simple and even naive approach to problems of mental disorder for which nowadays we have other names.[2] We may also discover in some of the miracle stories obvious symptoms of what we have come to call epilepsy.[3] But when that has been said, and when we have taken note of all the occasions in the gospels where we would find other descriptions for the sicknesses from which Jesus delivered men, it is at the same time necessary that we should not assume too easily that scientists nowadays believe (as they may well have believed less than one hundred years ago) that the universe is a rigid, fixed, and orderly affair with quite precise rules that *we* can discover, or that at least are capable of being discovered.

Most of us, if we pursue scientific studies far enough, are only too well aware of how many completely unexplained and apparently random pieces of behavior there are in this physical universe of ours. Furthermore, we have learned enough in the course of the last fifty years about the interplay of mind and body to know that there are whole areas of human sickness, mental and physical, that for reasons we are unable to discover do not respond in many people to the ordinary accepted ways of treatment. All of which is simply another way of saying that we have no right to dismiss the stories of healing in the gospels as either unscientific or in some way or other not worthy of our acceptance.

I want here to make one last comment. There were in the time of Jesus, or a little later, a great many "wonder tales" going the rounds, some of them frankly improbable or impossible, some of them incapable of proof, and some of them the kind of thing that perhaps to us would occasion no surprise. I refer to stories of apparently miraculous cures or miraculous escapes from death. But those are not, for the most part, anything like the kind of thing we encounter in the stories of healing in the four gospels. The "wonder tales" stand on their own; they are not intended and were not told as proof of any activity of God among men and seem on the whole simply to have been told for the sake of exciting comment and, as the name implies, "wonder." As a literary form they are quite easily recognizable to anyone with a classical education, and many of them must have been told many times over. It is hardly likely that the writers of our New Testament books would have been entirely unaware of the existence of these stories. But if we want a parallel to that kind of "wonder tale," we shall not find it in the miracle stories of Jesus. The best parallel to those old "wonder stories" is the kind of advertising that we get on television for various kinds of products, from deodorants to color television. I suggest to you that it might be worthy of a moment or two of your time to consider why we should find it comparatively easy to give complete belief to some of the wilder kinds of advertising and at the same time find it very difficult to accept some of the stories of healing belonging to the ministry of Jesus.

There is one event, of which there are several accounts in our four gospels, that took place during the ministry of Jesus and to which I suppose most people attach the word "miracle" without very seriously asking themselves what place the event occupied in the ministry of Jesus. Mark felt it to be so important that he told the story twice. I refer to the event commonly called "the feeding of the multitude." [4] In St. John's gospel this event is quite central and leads up to a long discourse by Jesus on the meaning of his own ministry, the meaning of his self giving to men and the meaning of his continuing presence with men. But there are several puzzles about it if we insist on taking the view that this story is simply concerned with a miraculous multiplication of bread and fish so that a crowd of hungry people was somehow or other miraculously fed in the desert. In point of fact there is a great deal more to it than appears on the surface.

For example, we have to ask ourselves what it was about this event that led men, that led some of the bystanders according to St. John's gospel, to wish to take Jesus by force to make him king. Nor is this all. We are, on the face of it, asked to believe that a hungry crowd—the numbers do not much matter—was not only filled, but the disciples afterwards picked up a very large quantity of fragments so that there was plenty left over. Is the story then simply an account of the use by Jesus of miraculous power so that a crowd of hungry people was fed and that there was plenty of food left over, presumably for another occasion? Perhaps we do not pay sufficient attention to some of the key words as they appear in all the accounts of the feeding. For example, if you would look carefully you will find that not only do the words "took," "blessed" (or gave thanks), "broke," and "gave" appear in all these accounts of the feeding of the multitude, they also occur in the accounts of the Last Supper in Matthew, Mark, Luke and also in St. Paul's account of the institution of the Eucharist, in 1 Corinthians, chapter 11. That should give us some useful insights into what was really happening at the feeding of the multitude. The idea may sound very strange to us, but one of the signs of the dawn of the Messianic Age for Jews of Jesus' own time was the belief that when the age of the Messiah dawned there would be a great feast, a Messianic banquet, which God would provide for his people.

What I want to suggest to you now is that the crowd that was with Jesus on the hillside understood perfectly well from what Jesus said in the giving of thanks, or blessing, that they were witnessing a dress rehearsal of the Messianic banquet. Nothing else really explains the desire of the crowd, as St. John records the incident, to take Jesus by force and make him a king. If the people there were firmly convinced that Jesus was indeed giving them a foretaste of the Messianic banquet, if Jesus in the course of giving thanks to God for creation and for the choosing of his people, Israel, made explicit reference to the future kingdom and to his own identification with it, that would have been more than enough to spark off a fervent nationalist desire to seize him there and then and proclaim him Messiah openly. There is then about this story a great deal more than meets the eye. But what of the pieces left over? Once again we must ask whether we really suppose that this was simply a straightforward account of Jesus' miraculous power to demonstrate his own care for his people. Or is there some other kind of interpretation that we can place upon the notice of fragments left over. Please note that it is St. Mark who tells us that Jesus pitied the crowd because they were "sheep without a shepherd." [5] The shepherd was a familiar designation for the king, the Messiah, and possibly here there is the hint given us by St. Mark of the meaning of the story he is about to tell. What seems to be said in St. Mark's rounding off of the story and its mention of fragments left over is the assertion by the Evangelists that in the Messianic kingdom there is enough and to spare for all men, that the life of Jesus, manifested to and given to men, is more than enough for all men's needs.

We have seen that, in terms of first-century Palestine, there is more to this story than meets the eye. So far as we Christians are concerned, who live nearly two thousand years after the event of this feeding of the crowd, we are to see in our own share in the Eucharist, our own participation in the Body and Blood of Jesus, and our own share in this with each other; we have indeed been invited to the banquet of the Messiah and our baptism—which gives us entrance into the kingdom—is also that which brings us into close association with Jesus so that we may feed on his life and grow closer to him and to each other.

Footnotes: [1] For example, Acts 2:22. [2] For example, Mark 1:23–27; 5:1–20. [3] For example, Mark 9:14–29. [4] Matthew 14:13–21; Mark 6:30–44; 8:1–10; Luke 9:10–17; John 6:1–13. [5] Mark 6:34.

12. jesus' understanding of his ministry

If the miracles were not intended to prove Jesus' claim to be the Messiah, then what did he say about himself? What titles are used of Jesus in the New Testament? The basis of all Christian belief is that, in Jesus, God declared himself, showed himself, once and for all and definitively. So far as God showing himself to men is concerned, the Christian claim is that in Jesus the summit of God's self-revelation was reached. But that was done in a very small country to one people, to the only people who were prepared for that kind of intervention in human affairs by God. The revelation took place, that is to say, within the framework of what we call "Judaism." And Jesus declared himself throughout his ministry in terms which were common to the Judaism of his times, terms inherited from our Old Testament scriptures. The name by which we refer most commonly to Jesus in our prayers and hymns, the word "Christ," is of course a Greek word that attempts to translate the Hebrew word "Messiah." I have referred to that word before now. It means "God's Anointed Servant," "God's Chosen Deliverer" and most commonly in the Old Testament refers to the reigning king.

Except in St. John's gospel Jesus does not refer to himself as Messiah at all.[1] Indeed, when he challenges his immediate circle of disciples as to the verdict which men are passing upon him, and the verdict they themselves pass upon him, he immediately silences Peter's reply that he is the Messiah, the chosen of God.[2] For that silence there are two reasons. First, the term Messiah had become associated in a good many people's minds with political revolutionary movements that could only be interpreted by the Roman authorities as subversive. Many pious Jews could only see such movements as being very far removed from the spiritual hope of God's reforming of men's minds and souls— which had been the hope of prophets in the Old Testament scriptures. There was, in other words, very grave danger of the word "Messiah" being used in ways that would have precipitated a blood-thirsty revolution and that would have effectively prevented the message of Jesus about the reign of God, with its demand for repentance, from ever being heard at all. Certainly this reason for Jesus' silencing talk about himself being the Messiah can never have been far from his mind.

But there was a second reason too. It is this: It seems clear that in the time of Jesus it was a common Jewish belief that the Messiah would not be known, or rather his identity would not be known, until it was declared by God. There are very good grounds for supposing that for some New Testament writers the identity of the Messiah, or the identification of the Messiah with Jesus in his ministry, was declared by God when he raised Jesus from the dead. There is, therefore, quite a legitimate way in which we may speak of the "secret of the Messiahship."

Perhaps it is well here to deal with the problem of the use of the term as it appears in St. John's gospel. This is particularly the case in St. John, chapter 4, where Jesus apparently not only spoke quite openly to a Samaritan woman about the hope of a coming Messiah, but declared quite clearly to her that he was that Messiah. This is not the place to go into all the reasons for one apparent exception to the secrecy which I have already outlined. But I want to say here quite simply that in my view Jesus on that occasion said to the woman of Samaria, "I am Son of Man." It was St. John, it was the evangelist, who supplied for the benefit of his readers the equivalent title of "Messiah" and put it on the lips of Jesus.

The term Jesus commonly used all through his ministry is the term, as it is translated in our Bibles, "Son of Man." This term, both in Hebrew and in Aramaic, has been a subject of discussion among Biblical scholars for very many years. It can mean one of two things. It can simply mean "a man" or it can mean a "man of authority." But within recent years, thanks to the recent manuscript discoveries associated with the Dead Sea Scrolls, it has become clear that we must begin to understand "Son of Man" as meaning "The Man" as though that phrase were in capital letters all the way through. It is not very easy for us to grasp the real content and meaning of the phrase, and we must do our best with what material we have. It means something like this: As long ago as two thousand years before the ministry of Jesus, men were talking of a restoration of man to his state of relationship with God or the gods by means of an intervention by a

heavenly being. Sometimes this restoration of relationship between God and men was expressed by saying that there would be
a return to a kind of "primal man," man in all his glory, man
without sin, man rescued by the intervention of a being from
heaven. That belief in one way or another persisted down the
centuries and it seems to be in that sense that some manuscripts
contemporary with Jesus (or in some cases prior to the time of
Jesus) used the term "Son of Man," or "The Man."

I think it will be a long time before we are able to use the
term "The Man" with the same kind of freedom with which we
have heard the term "Son of Man" as it has been read to us in
church. Nevertheless, there are various strands of folk tradition
in the United States where the term "The Man" has been consistently used for a very long time to mean someone in authority, and perhaps on that account Americans may be a little easier
with the term "The Man" than most Europeans would be. Jesus
uses the term "The Man" or "Son of Man" in three ways. First
he uses the term as meaning himself in the humility and the ob-
scurity of his earthly ministry.[3] Second, he uses the term as
applying to the "glory," the enthronement of his passion.[4] This
use is something to which we must pay attention a little later on.
Third, he uses the term "Son of Man" or "The Man" as meaning his glory and his majesty in judgment at the end of time.[5]
Now all these three uses have one thing in common. All of them
represent Jesus as speaking of himself in terms of *judgment*, with
himself as the judge. The coming of God's Representative
among men plainly faces men with a judgment. Men must
define what they are to make of this Representative in his apparent humiliation and in his apparent rejection. Judgment is something men most often pass upon themselves by their own attitude to things, events, and people. Then second, Jesus asks men
to see in his suffering, his passion and his death yet another judgment, for here too he is God's Representative; he is "The Man,"
he is "Son of Man."

The third way in which Jesus uses the term, that which refers
to judgment at the end of time, is much easier for us to grasp,

but in all three uses on the lips of Jesus the note of judgment is there all the time. When we read the New Testament, or when we hear it read in church, it is as well for us to remember when we hear the term "Son of Man," or "The Man," that Jesus sees himself as God's appointed judge.

Apparently in the time of Jesus this title was already passing into disuse. We find it in the Old Testament scriptures, principally in the writings of the prophet Ezekiel, referring to himself in his own position as God's Representative. It therefore has a lengthy history before we come to the ministry of Jesus.[6] But it is significant that outside the gospels the term "Son of Man" is used only three times in the New Testament—once in the Acts of the Apostles, chapter 7.[7] It was evidently disappearing from the theological vocabulary around the time of Jesus, and after his ministry seems to have not been used again in Jewish circles.

There is another title which Jesus used of himself, but since this calls for a little rearrangement of English translation in our gospels it will be necessary to pay a little more attention to it than often has been the case before now. You will find the title in Acts, chapter 7:52. There, the first martyr Stephen refers to Jesus as "The Righteous One." [8] Now this title is also ancient and appears to go back at least as far as the second century before the ministry of Jesus. It used to be thought that this title was only found in this solitary example of the Acts of the Apostles and nowhere else in the New Testament. But recently some attempts to look at the Greek of our New Testament with fresh eyes have produced other examples which up to now have been more or less hidden from view. We will stop to look at them, because that will help you to understand the kind of difficulty that we have when we try to translate New Testament Greek into English.

If you look at St. Matthew's gospel, chapter 10, verse 40, you will find that "anyone who welcomes you welcomes me, and those who welcome me, welcome the one who sent me." [9] That is straightforward enough. Then we come to the next verse, 41: "Anyone who welcomes a prophet because he is a prophet, will have a prophet's reward, and anyone who welcomes a holy man because he is a holy man, will have a holy man's reward." I don't know what you make of that verse 41, but it has always puzzled me to know exactly what is a prophet's reward and what is a holy man's reward. But if we remember that in the time of Jesus, Aramaic (and to a much lesser extent, Hebrew) had no definite article, had no "the," because the definite article was implied in the way in which the sentence was constructed, then you can begin to make some sense from that rather mysterious verse 41. It goes like this: "Anyone who welcomes The Prophet because he is The Prophet, will have a reward from The Prophet, while anyone who welcomes The Righteous One because he is The Righteous One, will have a reward from The Righteous One." Now that straightway makes more sense than our modern English versions do. What Jesus is saying is that here there are two kinds of expectations, two kinds of welcome being given to himself and to his mission. There are those who welcome him because they see in him The Prophet of the dawning reign of God. Those who welcome him, receive him as such, will be rewarded by that Prophet, by himself. But those who go further and see in Jesus "The Righteous One," the focal point of all the hopes of Israel, because they recognize him as "The Righteous One," will be rewarded by him, "The Righteous One." There are other uses of the term "The Righteous One" in the first letter of St. John, St. Matthew's gospel, and Peter's first Letter. The use of the term "The Righteous One" in John's first Letter (1 John 2:1) is quite familiar to those who use the Episcopal Prayer Book, where it comes in the Eucharist in what have come to be called "the Comfortable Words." The translation is, however, rather poor in all our versions and the Greek ought to be translated as follows: "If any man commits sin, we have an Advocate with the Father, Jesus the Anointed Righteous One." Properly understood the Greek will bear no other interpretation. Similarly, in 1 Peter, 3:18, we have "For the Messiah also died for our sins once and for all. He, The Righteous One, suffered for the unrighteous in order to bring us to God." The passage in Matthew 27:19 is difficult—not only because of a variant reading in some of our Greek manuscripts, but because of the person in whose mouth the term "The Righteous One" is placed. It reads: "Now as he was seated in the tribunal, his wife sent him a message: "Have nothing to do with that man, The Righteous One. All day I have been upset on account of a dream I had about him." Perhaps Pilate's wife had heard tell of Jesus under his title of The Righteous One, but it is very difficult to know under what circumstances that might have been. One thing is sure. The Greek word for "righteous" cannot mean, as some people have suggested for this context, "innocent."

It is quite evident to us now that this title, "The Righteous One," which was first applied in the Hebrew scriptures to Noah, then much later on to Simon the High Priest, was already dying out in the time of Jesus. Indeed, apart from Acts 7:52 and 22:14, the first Letter of John, the first Letter of Peter, and Matthew's gospel, we do not find it again in Christian literature. That does, however, suggest to us that Jesus was deeply steeped in, and had pondered very deeply over, the meaning of Messianic titles that were current in generations before his own. For all the fact that they were dying out in his own day, they seemed to him to suggest the best possible description of his message and his ministry. Perhaps above all else it is the title "The Righteous One," God's just and sinless Servant, that best expresses the ministry of Jesus to us. Perhaps the key passage in Jesus' own understanding of the term "The Righteous One" is to be found in the Hebrew of Isaiah 53:11—a passage upon which Christians have meditated long and often. Here it is from the Hebrew: "So he, The Righteous One, my servant, will vindicate the community." (The term "community," as a translation of the Hebrew, must be looked at again when we come to the account of the institution of the Eucharist.)

Then there is the title "Lord." This is extremely difficult to handle because the word for "Lord" in Greek, and in Aramaic, could mean a perfectly ordinary title of courtesy like "sir" or "Mr." But it is also the case that the word that is translated

"Lord" in our New Testament was being used by the Roman emperors to describe themselves as being in some sense divine. Some of Jesus' enthusiastic hearers and followers certainly applied the term as more than a courtesy title like "sir." We can get glimpses of the kind of thing I mean when we recognize that the first Christian credal statement about Jesus, "Jesus is Lord," apparently carries with it the assertion that Jesus is in some sense (perhaps only dimly) understood as being God. In other words, when St. Paul uses the statement "Jesus is *Lord*," he is probably using the word "Lord" in its Hebrew sense and not in its Greek sense, that is, he is saying the word Lord in this connection is the equivalent of the name of God, the person of God. (The word *Kurios*, Lord, is the word used in the Greek Old Testament to translate the Hebrew name for God.)

Every now and again in the gospel story Jesus is referred to as "Son of David," [10] but it is not clear whether Jesus accepted the title or not. Certainly it was a Messianic title and certainly anyone who belonged to the lineage, the ancestry, the tribe or "family" of David, would automatically in some sense or other be bound up with the old royal house. However, when Jesus is questioned about who he supposes the Messiah to be and turns the question back upon his inquirers, he apparently dismisses the whole question of Davidic descent as being of no more than historical interest. The old idea of the Davidic line was evidently felt by Jesus to be far too cramping and far too narrow a view of the ministry he had come to fulfill.

The term "Son of God" is applied to Jesus by St. Peter in the acknowledgement of Jesus' messiahship,[11] and here it is as well to remember that it is not used there in the sense in which later theology uses the term to describe Jesus' relationship to the Father. It would be perfectly clear to Peter that if he was acknowledging Jesus as Messiah, he was also acknowledging in *Old Testament* terms that the Messiah, the King, was the anointed Son of God in a particular and special fashion. After all, we ourselves are described in the New Testament as "Sons of God" [12] and "heirs of the Kingdom." [13] But for the Old Testament the anointed king, the Messiah, stood in a special relationship with God as God's vice-regent or, if you like, as God's deputy and the term "Son of God" seemed to express best someone who stood in an extremely close relationship to God for the people, and to the people for God. When we hear the term "Son of God" applied to Jesus by Peter we must beware of reading into it the kind of material that belongs to the later formulation of the creed we use at the Eucharist.

Footnotes: [1] John 4:25–26.   [2] Matthew 16:13–20.   [3] For example, Luke 9:57–58.   [4] For example, Matthew 17:22–23.   [5] For example, Matthew 16:27–28.   [6] For example, Ezekiel 2.   [7] Acts 7:56; Revelation 1:13; 14:14.   [8] From the New English Bible translation; The King James and Jerusalem Bibles render it "The Just One."   [9] Jerusalem Bible translation.   [10] For example, Matthew 9:27; Luke 18:38.   [11] Matthew 16:16.   [12] For example, Romans 8:14.   [13] James 2:5.

13. ends and means

Precisely what did Jesus come to do and how did he himself see the accomplishment and the fulfillment of his work?

The first part is easily enough stated: Jesus came among men to reconcile us with God. We have already referred to this in an earlier section of this Life of Jesus, and there is no reason to go over the same ground again. But even if we accept that there was a fundamental cleavage between men and God, formed by sin, it is still necessary to ask how that gap was to be bridged.

Jesus went around the countryside with the inner circle of his disciples, teaching them about God's kingdom and occasionally preaching and teaching to larger crowds of people. His teaching to the inner circle of the disciples is always a reassertion of God's purpose for men, laid out in terms of the choosing of Israel. Jesus, for example, accepts the validity of the law given to Moses. Jesus accepts the choosing, the election, of Israel by God as God's chosen instrument in the world for showing himself to men. I have already explained that the best way in which we can understand the ministry of Jesus as his contemporaries saw it is to understand Jesus as summing up in his own person all the history of his own people from Abraham down to his own time. Nevertheless, we have now to ask what sort of ideas men had about God's reconciling power, or God's response to the desire to be reconciled with God. Here we have to face what is admittedly something extremely difficult for us to understand. We have to try to enter into a world where reconciliation with God (where it was thought possible at all) was thought to be accomplished by means of sacrifice.

Sacrifice is a word with which we are perfectly familiar in church and in ordinary civil life. It is a term with which we are familiar in time of war, for example; but the word does not have for us the same kind of force that it had in days when animal sacrifice was an accepted part of man's approach to, and response to, God. Across practically every page of our Old Testament scriptures there is written a very large question: "If God hates sin, how can he possibly forgive it?" We do not very easily grasp the idea that for the Old Testament scriptures there was no *certainty* of forgiveness for sin. There was only *hope* that God would, in his mercy, forgive sin. Indeed, the Old Testament very often represents that hope as being very slender. There is, for instance, no possibility (according to the Old Testament scriptures) of any forgiveness for deliberate sin or as the Hebrew calls it "sin with an uplifted arm," "high-handed sin." At best there was forgiveness for accidental transgression, or forgiveness for ceremonial impurity. But for deliberate sin, the Old Testament can offer very little hope.

Animal sacrifice was offered once a year on the Day of Atonement, when the Temple priests sacrificed on behalf of Israel, in an attempt to bring the sins of the whole people before God. In addition, sacrifices were offered by individuals for the unintentional sins involved in a careless or unthinking performance of ritual religious acts or for something accidental, like walking over a grave. For sins that had been contemplated before their commission, there was no forgiveness possible. And yet the hope remained that God might forgive men, and men continued to

offer animal sacrifices for all sins. It is important for us to remember that the sacrificed animals were a precious part of a
man's livelihood, something that, in a real sense, represented his
very life and existence. It was as though men were saying something like this: "For deliberate sin there is apparently no certain
forgiveness and yet my sin will never cease until I die. I could, of
course, cut off sin in me by killing myself, but that is forbidden. I
therefore give to God what is extremely precious to me, what is
bound up with my very life and livelihood, in the hope that God
will look upon this part of me that I give to him, and forgive
me." That seems a rather simple way of explaining the reasons
behind animal sacrifice, yet Jesus grew up with that kind of attitude to sin and sacrifice and so far as we know he never questioned its validity for the past.

According to our New Testament sources, the life, ministry,
and death of Jesus very soon achieved their own sacrificial language. In St. John's gospel, for example, when Jesus came to him
John the Baptist said: "See, the Lamb of God, who takes away
the sin of the world." [1] Here at the very outset of the ministry of
Jesus is the language of sacrifice, the language of bloodshedding.
Now central to any understanding of the ministry of Jesus as the
New Testament sees it, and as Jesus himself saw it, is a long section of the second part of the Book of Isaiah the Prophet, chapters 40 through 53, where the whole problem of sin and God's
reconciliation with man is spoken of in language that is far more
familiar than we think: it has entered into our hymns and it is
used extensively in readings in church in Passiontide. These central chapters of Isaiah[2] speak of the possibility of God accepting
the total offering of a *representative* as giving back to God the
obedience that man was bound to offer but could not because of
sin.

But even so, the question remains: Did Jesus himself think of
his life, his ministry and death, in terms of a bloodshedding sacrifice, in terms of a total offering, a total giving to God, sealed
in death? There is in fact only one place in the ministry of Jesus
where he speaks clearly and without ambiguity of his total offer-

ing to the Father in terms of sacrifice. That occasion is the institution of the Eucharist, at the Last Supper. "This is my body which is given for you; this is my blood which is poured out for you." [3] Furthermore, the words Jesus used on that occasion speak of his blood-poured-out making a reconciliation with God by means of a new bond, a new covenant for the forgiveness of sins (an idea that looks directly back to Jeremiah chapter 31, verses 31–34). At that crucial moment in his ministry Jesus sums up his whole obedience to the Father—his whole ministry, his whole life, his whole work—and gives it the language of sacrifice. He seals his self-offering to the Father as summed up and shown to us in the bloodshedding of the cross. It will help you to understand a little of the language of sacrifice if you remember that what is important in animal sacrifice is not the killing of the victim but *what is done with the blood*. That is critical in Hebrew sacrifice, and our New Testament books speak in sacrificial terms of the "life," the blood of Jesus, being given to the Father on our behalf. Jesus speaks throughout his ministry in terms of total offering to the Father, of total self-giving, and all of that is understood, at the most critical point of his ministry, in terms of the "blood of sacrifice."

Footnotes: [1] John 1:29.   [2] The chapters in question were certainly not written by the prophet himself.   [3] Matthew 26:26–28; Mark 14:22–24; Luke 22:19–20.

14. the way to jerusalem

Jesus did a good deal of traveling up and down the country. We know very little about the *public* ministry of Jesus, and his private instruction to his inner circle of disciples, to the twelve, is preserved in epitomized form, rather like the "headlines" in our newspapers. It was not particularly strange for a teacher to collect around him a band of pupils and travel about the countryside for periods of time. As a matter of fact, we know a good deal from near-contemporary Jewish sources about the precise way in which these bands of teachers and pupils conducted their affairs. We know, for example, that when they were traveling on the road, pupils would follow at a slight distance behind their teacher; this may help you to understand why it is that Jesus asked his disciples at one point what they were talking about as they were journeying along the road together.[1] (This may have seemed to us as a little odd, since we would assume that they were walking with Jesus and he could overhear what they were talking about, whereas they were probably several paces behind him.) They would be accustomed to having their meals in common. They would occasionally, if they were in Galilee, earn enough money from fishing to keep them going for the next two or three weeks, but for the most part the time would be spent in discussing matters to do with the Law, with the hope and the prayer for the coming of the reign of God.

As we have seen, any talk in public or in private about the kingdom of God was potentially at that time a dangerous and explosive issue. It would have been impossible for Jesus to have conducted such a ministry without arousing the fiercest passions both of loyalty and of opposition. Our New Testament sources do not exaggerate when they represent people being in a ferment, wondering whether or not this person traveling with his pupils was, or was not, a nationalist Messiah like many who had gone before him, whether he was simply a dangerous fanatic, or whether in fact he represented a return to an older kind of Hebrew prophecy that spoke in stern and uncompromising terms of the judgment of God. That there were occasions of great gentleness and concern in the ministry of Jesus we know very well. Strange though it may appear to us, they can only have baffled or even in some cases enraged those who came in contact with him. Why not get on with the main business of preparing for the revolution? Why pretend that there is such a thing as a non-political Messiah? Why try to persuade anyone that the kingdom of God could come without bloodshed? And anyway, what *was* the attitude of this new teacher to the occupying Roman power?

There is nothing particularly strange about Jesus' own awareness of the way in which his ministry would end. There is nothing odd about Jesus prophesying his own violent death at the hands of his enemies, nor is there anything odd about Jesus deliberately seeking to be hidden for a time.[2] At all costs he had to make sure that those whom he was teaching were adequately prepared for the task which was to be theirs when his physical presence was no longer with them. What we have most clearly documented for us in our gospels is Jesus' last journey to Jerusalem.[3] As our gospels tell us, he deliberately set himself to go to Jerusalem. He deliberately set himself to go there, that is to say, when he knew that all that could be accomplished by means of teaching the twelve had been done. He must now give himself— and his disciples—into the hands of God. We do not know how long that final journey to Jerusalem lasted, but rumor went on very quickly ahead of him. By the time he came near Jerusalem, during Passover, one of the most emotional and sensitive times of the year for any Jew, there would be many who were seeking for him in the crowded city at Passover time.

St. John's gospel gives us a very vivid picture of enemies lying in wait; of simple people who had heard of Jesus and longed to see him; and of others torn between enthusiasm and doubt.[4] In the middle of it all was the vast mass of people who were coming to Jerusalem for Passover in their tens of thousands simply to keep the festival and wanting desperately to avoid any kind of confrontation with the civil power. It was just here, where we might expect the writers and compilers of our four gospels to be most careful over matters of chronology, that we are in fact in the middle of a very considerable confusion.

The beginning of the story is simple enough. We all know about the entrance of Jesus into Jerusalem on the first Palm Sunday,[5] but after that, we are in the middle of some very serious complications. On the traditional view, Jesus spent part of Monday, Tuesday, and Wednesday in and around the city, kept the feast of the Passover with his disciples on Thursday night, was arrested the same night and taken before the Jewish authorities and Pilate, and put to death early on Friday morning. But as a matter of fact any straightforward reading of our gospel accounts will soon convince us that if the traditional picture is true, then an enormous press of events took place between Thursday midday and the death of Jesus on Friday afternoon. There are several court appearances,[6] and in Luke[7] there is actually an appearance before King Herod. On top of all that the trial before Pilate seems to have been a quite protracted affair.[8] It is difficult to see how all the things our calendar traditionally associates with Thursday and Friday can possibly have been squeezed into the time available. But that is not the end of the matter. St. John's gospel represents Passover as beginning that particular year on Friday afternoon, so that Jesus died at the same time that the lambs for Passover were being slaughtered in the Temple.[9] In contrast, St. Matthew, St. Mark, and St. Luke[10] certainly seem to imply that Passover that year fell the day before.

What is one to make of all this confusion? The suggestion has been made in the course of the last fifteen years that in fact Jesus and his disciples kept a very old calendar that was not the calendar observed in the city of Jerusalem by orthodox Jews. The suggestion is that Jesus and his followers kept the old calendar of the Book of Jubilees, a calendar which we now know was kept by the Essenes (among whom, as we have seen, John the Baptist and even Jesus may have been brought up for a time). Very briefly, that calendar was a *solar* calendar, which may have been accepted among all Jews before the Babylonian exile of 586 B.C., whereas the calendar in general use among Jews after the return from exile was a *lunar* calendar. For the Essenes, Passover was always on a fixed day of the week, and *always* took place on a Tuesday night. It would be a very substantial undertaking to try to spell out all the ramifications of this suggestion, but it immediately relieves us of the tremendous sense of haste and the tremendous sense of overcrowding that the traditional view of Thursday/Friday chronology imposes upon us.

Using the Essene calendar, Jesus would have come into Jerusalem on the first Palm Sunday,[11] returned to Bethany on Sunday night,[12] come into the city on Monday,[13] and, on Tuesday, would have made preparations for Passover,[14] which he celebrated with his disciples. He would have been arrested on the night of Tuesday/Wednesday, and examined all day Wednesday in the ecclesiastical courts, with the Roman trial taking place on Thursday. In my opinion this chronology is much more acceptable than the traditional one.

Footnotes: [1] Mark 9:33.   [2] Mark 9:30–32.   [3] Matthew 20:17 to 21:11; Mark 10:32 to 11:11; Luke 19:28–44.   [4] John 11:45–57; 12:1–50.   [5] Matthew 21:1–11; Mark 11:1–10; Luke 19:29–38; John 12:12–15.   [6] Matthew 26:57–75; Mark 14: 53–65; Luke 22:66–71; John 18:12–14, 19–24.   [7] Luke 23:6–12.   [8] Matthew 27: 11–26; Mark 15:1–15; Luke 23:1–5, 13–25; John 18:28 to 19:16.   [9] John 19: 14.   [10] Matthew 26:17–19; Mark 14:12–16; Luke 22:7–13.   [11] See note 5.   [12] Matthew 21:17; Mark 11:11.   [13] Matthew 21:18; Mark 11:12, 15.   [14] See note 10.

glory

glory

15. palm sunday

The gospels agree that Jesus entered Jerusalem on the Sunday before Passover. The procession of disciples, with Jesus riding in the middle, which made its way from the Mount of Olives into Jerusalem,[1] would not have attracted much attention at first. After all, Jerusalem at the time of Passover Week was filled to suffocation with pilgrims from all over the world, and the sense of overcrowding is something from which our imagination shrinks. Perhaps the easiest way to visualize the situation is to imagine a city of some tens of thousands of people suddenly called upon to accommodate an influx of something like one or two hundred thousand people in its environs. Groups of people, neighbors or large families, certainly traveled to Jerusalem together, so that there would have been many small parties of pilgrims on the road to the city. In such a gathering, the small procession of Galileans with one man in the middle riding on a donkey can hardly have looked like the vast triumphal procession depicted in some of our stained-glass windows. It *is* clear, however, that the little procession caused a stir among Galileans who had come up for the feast. Recognizing Jesus by rumor (if not by previous knowledge of him) they began a patriotic demonstration, centering around the use of the word *Hosanna*, which is best translated as "Let salvation come now."

In the conditions of Palestine at the time, and in the conditions of Jerusalem at Passover, such a cry for divine intervention would have been enough to excite some parts of the festival crowd to a fever pitch. We know the demonstration swelled enough to provoke scornful attention from the Temple authorities and from Pharisees, who protested that the language employed by the demonstrators was not only exaggerated but also positively dangerous. Jesus went straight into the Temple. We are tempted to imagine the familiar story of the overthrowing of the money-changers' tables[2] as taking place inside something like one of our own church buildings. That would be totally mistaken. The Temple area was a complex of buildings with three very large courtyards surrounded by colonnades. The incident known to us as the "cleansing of the Temple" was certainly a symbolic act, but to those milling about in the courtyards it would have seemed at a distance to be no more than the kind of disturbance they had unfortunately learned to associate with Passover crowds. Without trying to downgrade the symbolic importance of what Jesus did, we should keep in mind the scale of this symbolic act of Jesus. We should also ask ourselves why this act of Jesus did not immediately provoke a full-scale riot and his immediate arrest. Having laid claim to his Father's house Jesus immediately left the city with his disciples and returned to Bethany.

So far as we can judge from our gospels, Monday was spent, after Jesus returned from Bethany, in a series of controversies with some representatives of official Judaism.[3] Nearly all the questions, nearly all the discussions, nearly all the attempts to trap Jesus into a position that would put him into the hands of the Roman authorities, concerned his right and his authority to speak and to act as he had done through his ministry. There were questions about his attitude to the Law of marriage; there were questions about whether or not he believed that it was lawful and right for a devout Jew to pay taxes to the Roman authorities, and above all there was the question about himself. Behind all the questioning there was the attempt to secure from Jesus some kind of admission that he was a political Messiah, that he had a political program and that he was proposing to act in some way contrary to the laws of either Judaism or the Roman civil authority.

When Jesus, months before, had stated quite plainly and bluntly that he would be given over into the hands of men, that is, into the hands of the authorities in Jerusalem,[4] he was simply stating the inevitable. Saying what he had said, acting as he had acted, there was only one possible end to his ministry: a head-on collision with one side or the other of Judaism. Jesus, in asking a question himself, "What do you think about John the Baptist?"[5] was not attempting to be clever or attempting to evade the question put to him. For Jesus, the ministry and work of John the Baptist were vitally important as an indication and a touchstone on the part of those who had heard John as to their attitude to the reign of God among men. Was John a prophet or was he not? Had he come with an authentic message from God, or was he a deluded fool? The question was turned aside by Jesus' critics, and Jesus must have known at that point that there was no turning back either for him or for them and that that Passover festival must inevitably end in his own violent death.

We can see a little of the way in which Jesus regarded this conclusion of his ministry when we turn to that rather perplexing story of his cursing the fig tree.[6] As the story has come to us, Jesus and his disciples were walking down a road on the outskirts of Jerusalem. Jesus caught sight of a fig tree on the other side of the road and went over to it, intending to pick some of the fruit, probably as a midday meal. When he got to it, he found that in spite of the broad-spreading leaves there was no fruit. As the story goes, Jesus promptly cursed the tree—he put the curse of God on it. The next day when they passed by the same spot, the fig tree was withered and dying. To us, the story as it is recorded sounds like pure spite or a rather oddly vindictive piece of behavior towards a tree which in any case could not make its own decisions about whether it had fruit or not. It is at least possible that what we have here is intended not as a literal story, but rather as a description of the way in which Jesus was thinking of his own people. The fig tree was a common symbol for Judaism among Jews. Jesus came with a message proclaiming the dawning reign of God; he came to his own people, the one people on earth who were expected to respond to such a message. But, in the words of St. John's gospel "He entered his own realm, and his own would not receive him." [7] Jesus comes to his own, to his own people, expecting that they will recognize what it is that he has to say, but on coming to Israel, to the fig tree, and expecting fruit, he finds it barren and dry. In a sense therefore the story of the fig tree is the story of the verdict of Jesus on his own people.

On the Monday and Tuesday after Palm Sunday the news would certainly have got into the highest circles in Jerusalem that this very troublesome teacher and preacher was in town, and the plotting which went on behind the scenes is only briefly indicated for us in our New Testament.[8] Central to the whole story is the figure of Judas Iscariot, the betrayer. We know very little of him save that he was a traitor, but it seems clear that there must have been something in Judas that appealed very much to Jesus when he was choosing the members of his inner circle. Perhaps Judas Iscariot had been a Zealot, one of those who passionately longed for the independence of Israel and the assertion of the reign of God. Perhaps having accompanied Jesus through the months of teaching he had become impatient with the way in which things were going; perhaps he had become totally disillusioned with the way in which Jesus proclaimed the reign of God; perhaps he sought by betraying Jesus to compel his teacher into some kind of rash political act. This would have sharply divided the people either for Jesus or against him but would in any case have brought to the very forefront all the burning issues of nationalism in that very divided country. These are speculations, and we cannot now know very much about what prompted Judas to agree to let the authorities in Jerusalem know where Jesus would be on a particular occasion. All we know is that some kind of agreement was reached, and that the time-serving authorities associated with the Temple clergy in Jerusalem were glad to have one troublesome problem apparently about to be removed for good.

Footnotes: [1] Matthew 21:1–11; Mark 11:1–10; Luke 19:29–38; John 12:12–15. [2] Matthew 21:12–13; Mark 11:15–17; Luke 19:45–46. [3] Matthew 21:23 to 23:39; Mark 11:27 to 12:40; Luke 20:1 to 21:36. [4] Matthew 16:21; Mark 8:31; 9:31; 10:33; Luke 9:22; 18:31–33. [5] Matthew 21:23–27; Mark 11:27–33; Luke 20:1–8. [6] Matthew 21:18–20; Mark 11:12–14. [7] John 1:11 (New English Bible translation). [8] Matthew 22:15; 26:3–5, 14–16; Mark 14:1–2, 10–11; Luke 19:47–48; 22:2–6; John 11:57; 13:2,27.

16. passover

On Tuesday, according to the calendar of the Book of Jubilees, Jesus and the disciples made preparations to keep the Feast of the Passover.[1] They made preparations to keep Passover, that is to say, according to the calendar of the Essenes. A description of the Passover meal is something you can very well look up for yourselves, always remembering that Passover among Jews nowadays has the same meaning that it had in the time of Jesus, but that it is no longer kept with a roasted lamb previously sacrificed in the Temple. That last Passover was a crucial moment in the life and ministry of Jesus. To begin with, Passover for the Jew commemorated, and still commemorates, God's great act in delivering his people from the slavery of Egypt and making of that horde of escaping slaves not only a people, but a people given to God in covenant and in Law.[2] Central to the keeping of Passover was the renewal year by year, by each person who kept it, of the knowledge that God had forged a holy people out of a rabble of escaping slaves. In addition, Passover looked to the future. It looked to the end of time, when God's rule, God's reign, would be known to all men, and when the whole natural order of the universe would be totally absorbed into the purpose of God. Of course for Jews in Jerusalem in the time of Jesus it had a very special significance, since in a very real sense the Jews were again almost enslaved and once more under

foreign domination. Knowing all that, the Roman authorities attempted to remain discreetly in the background during Passover.
Yet they heavily fortified the garrison in Jerusalem, and in the
surrounding towns, for always they were on the alert for anything which could turn into a national uprising.

For Jesus and his disciples as they gathered for this last celebration of the Passover together, the meal was to be the consummation of all the ministry of Jesus. He alone knew that, though
it is possible to gather from our New Testament sources that all
of them were aware of a tremendous sense of impending doom
and crisis. Now once again, while Jesus' enemies were busy plotting and the whole city was working itself up into a state of excitement and enthusiasm over the Feast of the Passover, and
when Jesus' friends were wondering where he was, Jesus himself
kept the great dramatic commemoration with his inner circle.

I must now return with you to the language of sacrifice, for it
is tremendously important in connection with the Eucharist that
Jesus instituted alongside the Feast of Passover. Jesus would
soon be in the hands of his enemies. Here, almost for the last
time, he was free to give himself totally to his Father for what
was to come. In the language of sacrifice he was, therefore, at
that Last Supper, High Priest; he was also Victim, in the sense
that he was deliberately offering *himself* to the Father for what
was to come. The seventeenth chapter of St. John's gospel has
Jesus speaking of "consecrating," dedicating himself, giving himself over completely to God.

The longer account of the Last Supper in St. Luke's gospel[3]
fits the scheme of the Passover very well—rather better, in fact
than the other accounts in St. Matthew[4] and St. Mark.[5] But at
what point in the Passover rite Jesus made the declaration as he
broke the bread and poured the wine: "This is my body; this is
the new covenant in my blood, which is poured out," we do not
know. The meaning is plain enough; it would run something like
this: "This commemoration in which you and I have taken part
brings into this present generation the life that God gave to our
fathers in the generations past. He will now, in a New Covenant,

give new life to you and to those who will follow you. The new life is enshrined in this act that you will do, for the life that God will give, as a result of my ministry, my suffering, and my death, is my own self. It is by me that you will live in this new Messianic community in the power of the Spirit. This then is my body broken, and my blood of the covenant poured out. This you will always do to bring back, bring into the present, something that for future generations will be a past event." Let us notice that *remembrance* and *memorial*, the words used in modern Eucharistic services, are very poor translations of the Greek original, anamnesis. The Greek word means "bringing into the present that which is past in time, and bringing it into the present by the effects of that past event." When God "remembers" in Biblical terms it is always to do something for his people, or to act on their behalf. Let us also notice that Jesus does not say "in remembrance of my death," it is "in remembrance of *me*." Each time you and I attend the Eucharist we bring into this present all the events of his ministry, his birth, his life among us; we bring into the present his total dedication to the Father, which was consummated in death and vindicated in Resurrection. That then, is the beginning of our Eucharist; that is the beginning of the Christian Passover. It is no longer an annual event, no longer a festival commemorated and performed once a year. The Eucharist belongs to every hour, to every day, and most especially to the day of the Lord's resurrection, Sunday.

When we come to deal with the Last Supper and the institution of the Eucharist, something must be said about the phrase "for many"—familiar to us from the Canon, or "Great Prayer," of the Eucharist. Why didn't Jesus say "for all men" (which is in fact the version used nowadays in English by Roman Catholics at the Eucharist)? We have constantly to remind ourselves that Jesus and his disciples were Jews, and that the admission of Gentiles to the Church was a matter which had to be thrashed out after the ministry of Jesus was over. "For many"—or, as it ought strictly to read, "for the many"—was (and still is, in the Jewish Prayer Book) a technical expression meaning "for the commu-

nity of Israel." It occurs, for example, in Isaiah 53:11, where we
have in Hebrew "My servant, the Righteous One will vindicate
the community." There are numerous other examples of the use
of the term in the New Testament, and it may be possible to examine those in another book. For the time being, we are concerned with the story of the ministry of Jesus in the gospels.
Here, at the Last Supper, he plainly states that the new covenant, sealed in his blood, is "for you—the Passover band of disciples (*chaburah* in Hebrew)—and for the community of Israel."
Primarily, as we have seen, his mission and ministry was within
the context of the worshipping community of Israel. How then,
if this interpretation of "for many" is correct, does that mission
and ministry come to us, who are Gentiles? St. Paul, who dealt
with the matter at length in some of his letters, *never* uses the
expression the "*new* Israel," however often he may refer to the
"new man in Christ" or the "new creation" or the "new age."
He is very much concerned to insist that Gentiles, who did not
belong to Israel by birth and circumcision, must be grafted into
the body of Israel as a shoot is grafted into a tree-trunk. He is always careful to remind the Gentiles that they have no call to
boast that *they* have accepted Jesus as Lord and Messiah while
the majority of Jews have not. After all, he says, God chose the
Jews, the Hebrews, as the instrument by which he would show
himself to the world—the Gentiles are accepted into the promises made by God to Abraham by grace, not by right.

When the Passover meal was finished, Jesus and his disciples
left the room where the meal had been eaten and crossed a
stream outside the city walls to go into a garden where they had
often been before.[6] There is one interesting piece of information
about the events in that garden that you ought to know. First of
all, understand that for purposes of keeping Passover it was not
considered necessary in Jesus' time, as it had been in the period
when Mosaic Law was written, to remain in one room or in one
house. Anywhere within the environs of the city of Jerusalem,
once the formal meal had been concluded, was reckoned to be
within the geographical limits set by Mosaic Law for purposes of

keeping Passover. Then you will recall that when Jesus and his disciples went into the garden, Jesus withdrew a short distance, leaving the disciples to keep watch while he prayed to his Father.[7] This episode, of course, describes Jesus in his total humanity, shrinking from the inevitability of a particularly terrible kind of death and seeking human companionship on the eve of his supreme trial. But another, contemporary, dimension of the narrative cannot be understood without reference to Passover customs that are not mentioned in the gospels. When Jesus came back for the first time to his disciples, he asked them a question that they were only just able to answer. They were sleepy, they were tired of watching. He came back in all, you will remember, three times. On the last occasion they were so tired and so sleepy that they could not answer him sensibly at all, and Jesus said "It is sufficient." This questioning, perhaps, is a little strange to our ears, until we know that the Passover meal was considered to be still going on, provided the youngest people who were at the meal were able to answer questions more or less sensibly. But when, in the course of the long-drawn-out celebration, questions were put to the youngest at the table, and the questions could not be answered coherently at all, it was reckoned that the meal was over. This is quite certainly the meaning which must be attached to Jesus' coming back to see if his disciples were awake or asleep. On the third occasion we must conclude that they were far too sleepy to answer sensibly or coherently, and that therefore for him and for them the Passover meal was at an end. It was time for Jesus' enemies to take over.

What, in the meantime, was Judas Iscariot doing? According to St. John he slipped out during the course of the celebration in the upstairs room, presumably to tell the authorities that Jesus and his friends intended to leave the house and go into the Garden of Gethsemane.[8] But before that there had been the rather puzzling incident of Jesus making the quite flat statement that someone at the table would betray him, and you will remember the questions that went round the table, each one questioning the other as to who it might be.[9] Jesus replied to John that it was someone who would be dipping with him in the dish of bitter herbs. That (as a sign that someone is a traitor) is puzzling, but again we have contemporary custom to help us understand what happened. Among the Essenes at any rate, the rules about taking food at table were quite precise. It was the seniors who were served first, and so on, down the ranks of seniority, until the youngest or the most junior. Anyone, therefore, who reached for food out of order was repudiating the authority of the leader, and his act constituted rebellion. It would seem that Judas reached out his hand at the same time as Jesus, and that although to one of the witnesses it looked as though Jesus was giving him something to eat, Judas was in fact at that moment repudiating the authority of his Master and teacher—and putting himself in a position of rebellion. This is only a guess, based on Essene custom, but it does make a rather bewildering report much easier to understand.

There remained for Judas only the final act of his rebellion—to go out and make the betrayal complete with the physical act of identifying Jesus for the arresting authorities.

Footnotes: [1] Matthew 26:17–19; Mark 14:12–16; Luke 22:7–13.   [2] Exodus 12:1 to 13:16.   [3] Luke 22:14–38.   [4] Matthew 26:20–30.   [5] Mark 14:17–26.   [6] Matthew 26:30–36; Mark 14:26–32; Luke 22:39; John 18:1.   [7] Matthew 26:37–46; Mark 14:33–42; Luke 22:40–46.   [8] John 13:27–30.   [9] John 13:21–26.

17. from this very moment

The scene in the Garden of Gethsemane as Jesus was arrested[1] is familiar to us all, and there is no need to repeat it here. What we must do now is follow the steps of the two trials of Jesus. It is very doubtful whether the appearance of Jesus before Annas and Caiaphas[2] was in the strictest sense a trial at all. It seems to have been an ecclesiastical examination to try to obtain from the lips of Jesus some damaging theological admission on which a major charge could be preferred to the Roman governor. There is a good deal of dispute among scholars as to whether or not the Jewish ecclesiastical courts in the time of Jesus were empowered to pass the death sentence for a capital offense under Mosaic Law. The whole narrative in our gospels suggests very strongly that the Jewish authorities were anxious to indict Jesus on some major charge that would be totally incapable of being misunderstood by any Roman civil governor. It is certainly the case that inscriptions in the Temple declared that anyone introducing a Gentile into the inner courts of the Temple would be condemned to death, presumably under Jewish law. But it was necessary in the case of Jesus to secure a charge, preferably sustained by an admission of Jesus himself, that would carry the utmost possible weight with the Roman governor.

The whole examination before Annas and Caiaphas sounds to our ears very confusing indeed, though it is well to remember that in Jewish courts there was no such thing as a defending counsel. There was a prosecutor, and the prisoner was left to defend himself as best he might. But after all the confusing testimony (some of it apparently contradictory) from witnesses who were far from disinterested, and who may even have been paid to give their witness, the high priest presented to Jesus the most solemn oath known to the Jewish law, an oath which charged the prisoner in the presence of the living God, to declare whether what was being said was true or not. The high priest's question was "I charge you in the presence of God, the living and the true, that you tell us whether you are, or are not, the Messiah, the Son of the Blessed One." In reply, Jesus refused again, as he had refused before, to answer a direct question that assumed that he understood "Messiahship" as the priests did. His reply to the high priest, "The words are yours," neither implies acceptance nor rejection of his vocation and ministry as Messiah. It simply rejects the interpretation that his enemies inevitably accused him of holding. Not even at that stage in the ministry would Jesus compromise his mission and vocation by answering a direct question that would have interpreted Messiahship in direct political terms. Jesus' reply, when it came, was one that no one could misunderstand—no one, that is, who had the least acquaintance with the kind of literature that had been circulating in some circles since the days of the Maccabean war in the second century before Jesus.

Jesus goes on to say, "But I tell you this: from now on, from this very moment you will see the 'Cloudrider,' The Man, seated at the right hand of God." There are a number of things involved in this reply, none of which succeed in coming through in our English versions, and this perhaps is one of those critical moments where our English translations, however good, demand a fairly adequate grasp of what lies behind the perfectly intelligible spoken word. Most of all, our English cannot adequately grasp the significance of the Greek in which our New Testament was written. When Jesus replies "From this very moment," you may remember that in the King James version the word used is "hereafter." That was perfectly intelligible in the seventeenth century as meaning "from this very moment," but in our ears sounds very strongly as though it means "some date in the perhaps distant future." The meaning was not lost, however, upon Jesus' hearers, and it certainly must not be lost upon us now. Jesus was inviting those who accused him to be witnesses to the triumph, the enthronement, the exaltation of The Man. So far, his words are plain enough. "From this moment on, this very moment, you will see The Man." What follows demands that we pay a little attention to a passage in the Book of Daniel, a book written or compiled to encourage those who were undergoing persecution during the Maccabean war of 165 B.C.

Daniel 7:13 has been the subject of a good deal of study among both Old and New Testament scholars for many years, and it is only now that the text is beginning to yield up some of the secrets of grammar and construction that lie behind the Aramaic in which it was written. The translation which I give here is one that I do not propose to defend to you, even though it differs quite widely from that given in our modern English translation. It was the result of some study done by Professor Wil-

liam F. Albright and myself quite recently and the work that
went into it must appear elsewhere. Here then is the translation:

In the night I saw visions:
See how the Cloudrider, The Man, comes to the Lord of Time!
And they bring him near before him.

Very obviously those who heard Jesus make this reply were familiar with Daniel and understood it as it is translated here. The
reaction to this statement by Jesus that they would see almost
immediately the triumphal enthronement of The Man was violent—though from the point of view of his critics predictable.
We would say that they ranted and raved, though in the circumstances of the time their ranting and raving was a symbolic ges-
ture—tearing their clothes—at hearing words they condemned
as blasphemous. Jesus was equating himself with the Cloudrider,
The Man, the one brought to the Lord of Time to receive a
kingdom, dominion, and glory. It is very difficult in the light of
this to understand how the high priest and those on the council
(from their own point of view) could possibly have reached a verdict in any other way than they did, that is, that Jesus was guilty
of blasphemy in claiming to be the Cloudrider, The Man. He
was judged to be worthy of the death sentence.

Those who had sought to deliver Jesus by some means or
other into the hands of the secular Roman authority finally had
something to go on. It was perfectly possible to hand Jesus over
to the civil Roman authority and accuse Jesus of planning treason against the Roman emperor by setting himself up to be a
king. So Jesus was taken to the prefect of the province of Syria,
Pontius Pilate, who later became the procurator of the province.
The accusation was simple: the prisoner was guilty of plotting
against the Emperor. Doubtless there were a good many people
present at that scene who equally might have been accused of
plotting against the Emperor, people who at one time or another had taken part in various clandestine schemes to rid the
country of the hated occupying authority. Perhaps too there

were those who hoped, on the basis of what they had heard about Jesus, that even at the eleventh hour sheer force of circumstance would compel Jesus to assert his Messianic power by some prodigious display of miraculous powers. But we may suppose that, for the most part, those who were in Jerusalem and were aware of what was going on either were simply bewildered or else dismissed the affair out of hand as yet another Galilean agitator being brought to justice. It is important not to overlook the fact that at that time Jerusalem was a very, very crowded city, and undoubtedly the vast majority of people simply wanted to be left alone to enjoy the Passover holiday and the religious celebration that enshrined the holiday.

It is important that we do not exaggerate the numbers of people who would have been aware of the taking of a prisoner from the scene of the Jewish council to the court of the prefect of the province.

Footnotes: [1] Matthew 26:47–56; Mark 14:43–52; Luke 22:47–53; John 18:3–11.   [2] Matthew 26:57–68; Mark 14:53–65; Luke 22:54, 66–71; John 18:12–24.

18. crucifixion

There are two main accounts of Jesus' appearance before Pilate, one given by the synoptic gospels,[1] the other by St. John.[2] The impression given by the gospel of John is that the examination was somewhat more leisurely than appears to have been the case from the other three gospels—though it is worth bearing in mind that Luke represents Jesus as having been sent by Pilate to Herod, who was in Jerusalem at the time.[3] It is, however, equally possible that the details given by Luke of Jesus' appearances before Herod and Pilate are somewhat confused. Be that as it may, Pilate emerges from our gospel sources as a very bewildered man.

The impression generally given to us, sometimes in sermons, is that Pilate was a coward. That does not do adequate justice to his character, for generally he seems to have been no better, and certainly no worse, than any other Roman administrator in a fairly distant province. Moreover, Pilate very seldom gets credit for his undoubted desire to calm a situation which might easily have gotten out of hand, one that could have turned Jerusalem into a shambles at a time when it was already difficult to preserve order amid a mass of converging pilgrims. It is certainly true that Pilate, especially in St. John's account, seems to vacillate and to hesitate about the advisability of subjecting Jesus to savage and cruel punishment by flogging and then letting him go, or alternatively of giving way to those who demanded the death of Jesus. The details of Jesus' examination before Pilate are probably very familiar to you, and you may read them for yourselves again in the accounts given in the gospels. Our own sense of shock is probably somewhat misplaced when we contrast the behavior of the crowds who accompanied Jesus into Jerusalem on Palm Sunday with the behavior of the crowds as they appeared outside the courtroom of Pilate. For one thing, anyone who follows the newspapers should need no lessons about the fickle behavior of a mob and the way in which the enthusiasms of a crowd can easily be turned from one object of hate to another, almost at the drop of a hat. But we may doubt whether the crowds who accompanied Jesus into Jerusalem on Palm Sunday (perhaps the majority of whom were Galilean) were anything more than feeble spectators on the edges of a bloodthirsty mob screaming for Jesus' death on that Thursday night/Friday morning. We have no idea how many people were present there when the prisoner was brought to Pilate. It may not have been more than one or two hundred, but sufficiently encouraged and sufficiently enthused by their leaders (among whom were undoubtedly members of the aristocracy in Jerusalem), it was not too difficult to make it appear to Pilate that the whole population was demanding the death penalty. (Does this sound somewhat familiar in terms of today's "demonstrations" as shown in newspaper and television pictures?)

Unquestionably the one thing uppermost in Pilate's mind when he passed sentence was the fear that after all it might be true that the stained and dirty figure before him had indeed been plotting treason against the Roman authority. For all the conflicting evidence, for all the shouts of the mob, for all the evident signs there were many there acting simply out of venom, Pilate probably concluded that in some way or other he had to play safe. He therefore condemned Jesus to be flogged and then crucified.

Many prisoners died under a Roman flogging, which was of a cruelty and a savagery which not even our own generation has been able to surpass. Perhaps here too, as we may see from reading the gospels, there has been some confusion in the minds of the evangelists as to whether Jesus was flogged before sentence of crucifixion was passed or whether the two sentences went together. But whichever way it was, Jesus was flogged, mocked by tense, tired soldiers with no particular desire to take part in an execution in the middle of a festival that was already potentially dangerous.

Christian piety has dwelt with great longing and great love on the journey of Jesus to the cross. It has dwelt on the agony of men's souls as they contemplated the result of sin in the blood-pouring of the death of Jesus. I shall not here go into the details of crucifixion—they are well enough known.[4] It was by no means a new punishment, for the Romans had simply inherited it, along with a good many other forms of punishment for non-citizens, from the Middle East. The victim so condemned generally carried the cross-beam of his own instrument of death with the title of his accusation hung on a placard round his neck. It seems to have been common practice for Romans to leave the upright parts of crosses in places of execution as a permanent reminder. You will probably know that the victim was either nailed or roped to the cross (or both), the nails being driven through the wrist and heel bones with a small foot-rest and a very small saddle to support the body. The victims often took as long as two or three days to die, and we have been assured more than once by medical evidence that death took place as a result of suffocation. The sordid details of it all we can probably conjure up for ourselves.

When all the details have been imagined, the central fact about the crucifixion is that Jesus accepted it as the final act in his own self-giving to the Father for us. It is the consummation of a life of total obedience freely given. It is almost painfully easy for us to repeat phrases like "a life of total obedience" or "freely given" and we have dealt before with what Christians mean when they talk about the sinlessness of Jesus. We can therefore only imagine what this sinlessness must have meant as Jesus came to his death.

Footnotes: [1] Matthew 27:1–2, 11–25; Mark 15:1–15; Luke 23:1–7, 13–25. [2] John 18:28–40. [3] Luke 23:8–12. [4] Matthew 27:26–56; Mark 15:16–41; Luke 23:26–49; John 19:1–30.

19. death

Death is something from which we all shrink. It is one of these moments in life, perhaps the supreme moment, when we are (at any rate in the closeness of our own minds and souls) entirely alone. It is an adventure upon which we must enter completely alone. Jesus embraces death, but along with the giving of himself at that final moment when most men shrink from giving of themselves, there went also the realization that that was the supreme blood-pouring for the sins of men. It is very easy for Christians to repeat phrases such as "Jesus took away the sin of the world" or "Jesus redeemed us from sin." As we now think of the crucifixion it is worth a moment to examine what such phrases may mean. If you can imagine yourself coming to your prayers at night and examining your conscience and discovering that you were responsible, in your own person, not only for your own sins but also for the sins of every man, woman, and child in the whole state for all of twenty-four hours, then I think you will conclude that this is almost beyond any kind of imagination. Yet as Jesus in this final moment of self-giving, meditated upon, and spoke aloud, words from Psalm 22 [1] we may very dimly imagine what sin meant to someone who was completely sinless. He gives himself to God, sinless, but bearing all human sin. We cannot know what horror that must have presented to his soul and mind. We can only turn over in our minds that it drew even from his lips the beginning words of Psalm 22, "My God, my God, why have you deserted me?"

Jesus, according to St. John's gospel, came to his death shouting the words "It is consummated! It is ended!" [2] That was not an expression of despairing resignation in the face of the inevitable. It was a triumphant assertion that at the end he had fulfilled what he came to do. There is one note here which must be added for the sake of clarity—and also by way of preliminary to any future study of the early part of the history of the Christian church in the New Testament. It is this: St. John's gospel tells us that as Jesus died, "he gave up the spirit." [3] That is the translation with which we are most familiar, but in several ways I doubt if it is really adequate. The words employed by St. John in Greek can certainly mean "He handed over" or "delivered over" the Spirit. In other words, the death of Jesus released that promised Counselor who would be the presence of Jesus the Lord in his household the Church when his visible presence was removed from this earth. We shall examine this thought later on; for the moment I ask you simply to bear in mind that the words in St. John's gospel *can* mean (and in my view certainly *do* mean) "He delivered over the Spirit." The final act of obedience on the part of the ministering Servant, the suffering Messiah, made it possible for there to be born even at the moment of his death the community of the new Covenant, the community that was to be indwelt by the spirit of God.

It has been suggested from time to time by non-Christians that Jesus did not really die, that in some way or other he was resuscitated by the cold air of the tomb in which his body was laid. The plain evidence of the gospel story as it is written for us in

our New Testament books certainly had no interest in proving
anything of the kind about the death of Jesus. The writers are
perfectly clear that he had died. Indeed, you will remember that
St. John's gospel tells us of the undoubted relief the soldiers felt
when they could report that at least one prisoner was dead and
so had that much less to worry about in the middle of the hectic
confusion of the Passover festival.[4]

With the details of the burial of Jesus we shall not here be
concerned;[5] it is more important for us to consider one theological point of very great significance. It is this: when Jesus came
near to his cross, came near to being delivered to his enemies,
did he, or did he not *know* with certainty that he would be
raised from the dead? It is true that the predictions of Jesus
about his Passion and death are all represented to us in the New
Testament as having Jesus plainly state that he would be raised
from the dead. We can consider these sayings as words by which
Jesus gave himself in total faith and confidence into the hands of
his Father. Did Jesus *know* that he would be raised from the
dead? From time to time in this life of Jesus we have talked
about Jesus as Man, Jesus growing up in all respects like you and
me. Now there is all the difference in the world between complete certitude and an act of faith. When you and I say "I believe in one God," or "We believe in one God," we are saying
"We commit ourselves in total trust to God." If Jesus had
known, with absolute and final *certainty* that he would be raised
from the dead, then to that extent there would have been that
much lacking in his abandonment in faith to his Father. Once
again we are dealing with Jesus as Man. We are dealing with
total humanity, giving itself in total trust and total abandonment to the Creator. In such trust and abandonment Jesus
comes to the moment of his death trusting to be vindicated by a
righteous Father. It is no use claiming that Jesus was simply a
very good man. Certainly he was that, but there have been a
great many very good men who have been cruelly and savagely
done to death. There will undoubtedly be a great many more
very good, very honest, very holy men who will be savagely and

brutally done to death by their enemies before the history of this planet is over. That is simply not enough. If Jesus was, as he himself understood himself to be, The Man, total representative Humanity, bearing for all men everywhere forever the appalling consequences of human sin, then, if he died and remained dead, there is no possible hope left for us, no possible joy, and certainly no possible love in being concerned for other people, and certainly there is no possibility anywhere at all of an ultimately good outcome of anything evil.

Jesus died, and if he remained dead, then (as St. Paul remarked) all human hope is baseless and a mockery.[6] Remember, please, that here I am speaking to Christians. There are many who must regard, and do regard, Jesus as a holy and a dedicated person, but who certainly do not believe that he was either Representative Humanity or still less that he was God in human flesh. For them it is possible to regard Jesus as a martyr to misunderstanding or misrepresentation, or even the victim of power politics. For us who have committed ourselves in trust not only to God as Creator, but to Jesus as God's final and definitive revelation of himself to us men, then that verdict simply will not do. That is what lies behind what Christians know as the Resurrection.

Footnotes: [1] Psalm 22:1; Matthew 27:46; Mark 15:34.   [2] John 19:30.   [3] John 19:30.   [4] John 19:31–34.   [5] Matthew 27:57–60; Mark 15:42–47; Luke 23:50–56; John 19:38–42.   [6] 1 Corinthians 15:12–19.

20. resurrection

Do not be surprised, since academic scholars are not, that the accounts of the raising of Jesus to life in the New Testament[1] differ from each other in sometimes quite startling ways. If all the accounts of the raising of Jesus agreed in every minute detail then I think we would have every good reason to suspect that the authors of those accounts, or those who handed on their tra-

dition to the writers, had all been guilty of a very great deceit
and fraud, and of active collusion with each other in perpetrat-
ing that fraud. In broad outline the stories are the same. In
broad outline we have the first bewildered visits of those who
went to see the grave after Jesus had been buried, only to find it
empty. There are, in broad outline, stories of Jesus appearing to
his disciples and to those who had been intimately associated
with him during his ministry.[2] But in *detail* all of them differ.
What emerges from all the differing accounts is that the writers
and those who first told the stories to each other were bewildered beyond belief (St. Mark says "they were afraid")[3] by what
had happened. They were bewildered by a sudden reversal, bewildered by an act of God that suddenly had overturned all the
horror and all the fears. In ways which they could not compre-
hend, he was alive again. In ways which they could not fully describe, he was alive and yet was very different. In ways completely beyond their powers of description he could appear and
disappear at will, he belonged to them again and yet very obviously did not belong to them. He appeared in the familiar
scenes of his ministry once more, and yet he was no longer tied
to the scenes of that ministry.

It was here, in what was once described as "the arena of our
sweat, blood and tears," that Jesus died, was buried, and was
raised. It was here on this earth that the hope of men underwent
and accepted all that the sin and the despair of men could inflict
upon him, and was raised triumphant over it. This is the message
of the Resurrection, simply stated. It is the resurrection of hope,
it is the raising again of the dignity of humanity. It is well here
to notice that the authors of our New Testament books in describing the raising of Jesus are quite precise in saying that God
"raised him from the dead," or "He was raised from the dead."
The act of resurrection was God's vindication of his Righteous
Servant; it was God's acceptance of the total offering of the obedient Son. This act of resurrection was not something that lay in
the inner strength of spirit of a single man. It was God's judgment upon a humanity re-created in Jesus; it was God's accept-

ance of that re-created humanity. It is for Christians at one and
the same time the answer to all hope and all longing. At the
same time it is also judgment on human sin. In hymns and in
prayers we speak, rightly, of the immense "price" which God
paid in order to re-create the human race, potentially, in Jesus.

One more rather significant passage in St. John's gospel demands our attention.[4] The story represents Mary Magdalen
looking with anguish and distress at the empty tomb of Jesus.
Not recognizing him she asked where the body had been taken.
How often has it occurred to you to ask why Mary did not recognize Jesus? Have you ever asked yourself how Jesus, who had
been very hurriedly wrapped and buried in a long winding sheet
almost certainly covered with the blood and the dirt of his
death, was not recognized by Mary? She did not recognize him
for the perfectly simple reason that he appeared to her clean and
clothed, and she very rightly and properly mistook him for one
of the attendants in the gardens near the tomb. This, to begin
with, illustrates one very important truth about the resurrection
of Jesus. His resurrected body was totally different from his body
as his friends had seen it on the night of his death. When Jesus
spoke Mary's name and she recognized him, Jesus replied,
"Don't go on hanging on to me. Go and find my brothers and
tell them, I am ascending to my Father and to your Father, to
my God and to your God." Mary Magdalen was being told that
the old earthly fashion of Jesus' ministry was ended. He belonged to that kind of ministry no longer. "Do not go on hanging on to me." But then he goes on to say "I am ascending to my
Father and your Father."

Many people are worried by the resurrection of Jesus, worried
by questions such as, "What kind of body did he have?" or,
"Did he eat and drink?" Or sometimes the question is put like
this: "*How* did God raise him from the dead?" Some people simply say "I don't believe it, because no one else has ever been
raised from the dead."

Many of the questions are really failures to face up to the assertion the New Testament, and our faith, make about the resur-

rection of Jesus—that it was unique. Consider for a moment: *If* Jesus was God in our human flesh, *if* Jesus was the new humanity totally given to God, *if* Jesus was a new beginning to the human race, *if* (to sum it all up) Jesus was Representative Man, then what possible evidence *could* we have from elsewhere? However much you might admire Jesus, or admire some of the things he did and said, here you are up against the bedrock upon which Christian faith and hope rests. Here you have to make the quite firm commitment of faith, which says, "I believe, I trust in him, risen and glorified," or you cannot be a Christian. There are no possible half-way houses here. Either the record is true, for all the bewilderment of those who tried to express it in words—or Jesus was a liar, and was so all through.

The New Testament writers themselves are at a loss to say precisely what *kind* of body the resurrection body of Jesus was. That he could come and go at will is underlined for us by St. John's gospel very firmly,[5] while St. Luke's version is so anxious that we shall understand that it *was* Jesus and not a phantom of the imagination whom the disciples saw that he has incorporated a tradition of Jesus sitting down to eat with the disciples.[6]

We are not able to draw upon either experience or imagination to deal with this—we are left with the startled record of men who had seen him and were baffled to know how to describe something for which no amount of previous thinking or upbringing had prepared them. Dimly, many men had been convinced that in some way men do survive physical death, though in what way was totally unknown. Some later books of the Old Testament had spoken of resurrection, but Jesus had spoken of it openly as referring to himself. No amount of "ghostly" visitation, no amount of "spiritual awareness," would have convinced the disciples that Jesus had been raised if he had not appeared to them. The disciples have left us their own sense of utter astonishment at the reversal, the total reversal, of all that had happened on Good Friday.

It may well be that the most convincing "proof" of the raising of Jesus from death, and his appearances to the disciples, must come from any attempt to explain how frightened men, who had deserted him at the last, suddenly became men utterly without fear, facing the world with a proclamation that he had been raised from the dead. We may reflect upon the ridicule that met their proclamation, and ask ourselves whether they were right or wrong.

We are so accustomed and conditioned by our liturgical calendar to suppose that there was a long period between Jesus' resurrection and his last appearance to his disciples that we fall into the trap of supposing that Jesus after his resurrection lived in a kind of half world belonging neither to earth nor to heaven; then we go on to assume that at the end of that long period there was a more or less dramatic scene in which Jesus was parted from them, gradually disappeared from sight into the clouds, and returned to heaven.[7] But the present tense which is used by St. John, "I am ascending to your Father and my Father"[8] should give us sufficient indication of what St. John is trying to say. He is telling us in the clearest terms possible that the vindication, the glorification, the exaltation of Jesus the Messiah to the Father, to the throne of the Godhead, was all of one piece. His glorification was his passion, his crucifixion, his death, and his rising again. A twelve year old girl in a catechism class once put this as well as it can be said when she asked the question, "Where was Jesus after his resurrection when he was not appearing to his disciples?" Very obviously the answer to that question is, he was with his Father. What I am trying to say is that we must try to take into our minds that this great act of God at the end of the ministry of Jesus is one thunderclap of triumph, all comprehended in the moment of the raising of Jesus. It is at one and the same time the Father's vindication of his Son, the Son being received by his Father and his ministry accepted, and also the gifts of the indwelling Spirit to the church. If we go on to ask "Why then did St. Luke at the end of his gospel and also in the first chapter of the Acts of the Apostles write an account of an ascension apparently forty days later?" then I think we must be grateful to St. Luke for giving us an occasion to take in one thing at a time. It is almost beyond our human imagining to think now of celebrating crucifixion, resurrection, ascension, and the gift of the Spirit to the Church all in one great broad sweep of one festival. But that is apparently what early Christians did, and the Feast of the Ascension is very much a latecomer on the Christian scene, dating from the fourth century. Perhaps St. Luke has "theologized" (which is a word academic scholars are rather fond of using) the last appearance of Jesus to his disciples. Whether that took place ten days, twenty days, thirty or forty days after the raising again, we do not know. We do know that Jesus appeared frequently to his disciples, apparently without warning. St. Luke is apparently trying to deal with the bewilderment they felt (of which St. John's gospel too has echoes) when they realized that those appearances had terminated for ever.

That then is the triumphant conclusion to a life triumphantly lived and a life triumphantly living still within that body of the faithful that we call the Church. The events of the life, ministry, death, and rising again of Jesus are many years removed from us. Yet the faith of the Church is, and the faith of the New Testament is, that the life, ministry, death and rising again of Jesus are being lived out in each one of us. We are taken into the community he founded, we are taken into this Body of Christ, this Church, this household of God, one by one, and in that household, that Church, that Body, each one of us is given the responsibility and the task of living more and more closely knit to that life, ministry, death, and rising again of Jesus. Jesus, in the power of the Spirit, takes us into the Father's household as sons in the Son. We are fellow heirs with him of the glory of heaven. We are, here and now, sharers with him in eternal life with the Father and the Spirit. St. Paul calls this Christian life of ours a first installment. Death, because he died, and was raised, is no longer deadly for the Christian. Death is what God all along meant death to be—a transition from a life of union to a life of a closer union with him. The reward for loving God is to love him better.

What we have been trying to do is look at this life, ministry, passion and resurrection of Jesus in the most straightforward terms possible. What the early Christian writers in our New Testament made of the life and ministry of Jesus, how they debated about its meaning, how they tried to draw out its implications in terms that were familiar to their hearers, is something which we may well leave for another occasion. It remains simply to be said that for you, for me, and for all Christians, the baptized eucharistic life in the Church, in the household of God, in the Body of Christ, is that for which all men are born and that to which all men are called.

Footnotes: [1] Matthew 28:1–8; Mark 16:1–8; Luke 24:1–12; John 20:1–18. [2] Matthew 28:9–10, 16–20; Mark 16:9–18; Luke 24:13–49; John 20:19 to 21:25. [3] Mark 16:8. [4] John 20:14. [5] John 20:19 to 21:25. [6] Luke 24:42–43. [7] Mark 16:19; Luke 24:50–51; Acts 1:1–11. [8] John 20:17.

chronology

1850–1550 B.C. Age of Abraham and the Patriarchs. Egypt a major power throughout Old Testament period. Other world powers include Hittites, Mari, and (until 1950 B.C.) Ur.

1700 (?) B.C. Hebrews in Egypt.

1280 (?) B.C. Exodus under Moses.

c. 1250–1200 B.C. Conquest of Palestine under Joshua and others. Hittite empire ends. Egypt in a state of weakness.

1200–1020 B.C. Period of the Judges ("Deliverers"). Time of Deborah and Gideon. Egyptian empire ends, 1100 B.C.

After 1051 B.C. Fall of Shiloh and destruction of the Shrine of the Ark. Samuel. Philistine settlement in Palestine begins.

1020–1000 (?) B.C. Saul, first king.

c. 1000–961 B.C. David.

c. 961–922 B.C. Solomon. Syrian kingdom begins.

922 B.C. Division of Israel into two kingdoms, Judah in the south (capital at Jerusalem) and Israel in the north (capital later established at Samaria).

869–850 B.C. Ahab, king of Israel. Elijah and Elisha. Assyrian recovery begins.

c. 750 B.C. Amos and Hosea, prophets to Israel.

720 B.C. Northern kingdom destroyed by Assyria—mass deportations.

c. 740–688 B.C. Isaiah and Micah, prophets to Judah.

625–586 B.C. Jeremiah, prophet to Judah. Zephaniah and Nahum, prophets, about the same time. Babylonian power grows.

597 B.C. First attack on Jerusalem by Babylonians. Deportations.

586 B.C. Sack and fall of Jerusalem.

582 B.C. Third deportation from Judah. Persian power grows.

550 B.C. Persians overthrow Babylon. Second part of Isaiah, by an anonymous prophet. Ezekiel also written around this time, partly in Judah and partly in Babylon.

538 B.C. Edict of Cyrus, king of Persia, allows Jews to return to Palestine. Egypt under Persian rule.

520–515 B.C. Temple rebuilt. Prophets Haggai, Zechariah, and (probably) Obadiah.

458 (?) B.C. Visit of Ezra to Jerusalem. Second visit in 428 (?) B.C.

445 (?) B.C. Nehemiah, governor of Judah.

336–323 B.C. Alexander the Great.

323–285 B.C. Jews under the Ptolemies (Egypt).

200 B.C. Conquest of Palestine by the Seleucids.

167 B.C. Profanation of the temple under Antiochus IV.

166–160 B.C. Judas Maccabeus. Rise of Roman power in Eastern Mediterranean.

164 B.C. Rededication of the temple. Rise of the Hasidim ("The Devoted Ones") and the Essenes.

63 B.C. Beginning of Roman rule in Palestine.

43–4 B.C. Reign of Herod the Great.

6 (?) B.C.–A.D. 30 (?). Life of Jesus.

4 B.C.–A.D. 39. Herod Antipas, Tetrarch of Galilee.

A.D. 27–37. Pontius Pilate, Procurator of Judaea.

A.D. 51. Council of Jerusalem.

A.D. 66. Beginning of Jewish revolt against Roman rule.

A.D. 70. Fall of Jerusalem to Romans. Final destruction of the temple. End of the Jewish state as such.

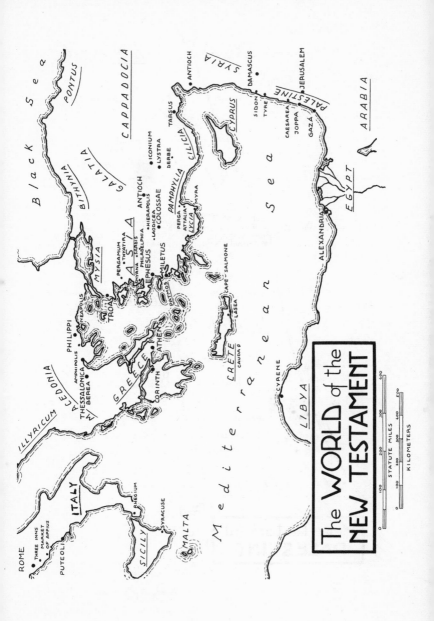

The WORLD of the NEW TESTAMENT

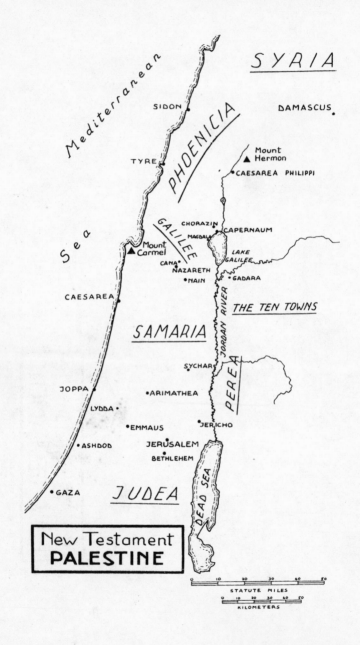

Mediterranean

SYRIA

SIDON •

DAMASCUS •

PHOENICIA

TYRE •

Sea

▲ Mount Hermon

• CAESAREA PHILIPPI

GALILEE

CHORAZIN •

CAPERNAUM •

MAGDALA •

▲ Mount Carmel

LAKE GALILEE

CANA •

• NAZARETH

• NAIN

• GADARA

THE TEN TOWNS

CAESAREA •

SAMARIA

JORDAN RIVER

SYCHAR •

PEREA

JOPPA •

• ARIMATHEA

LYDDA •

• EMMAUS

• JERICHO

• ASHDOD

JERUSALEM •

• BETHLEHEM

DEAD SEA

• GAZA

JUDEA

New Testament PALESTINE

0   10   20   30   40   50
STATUTE MILES

0 10 20 30 40 50
KILOMETERS